LET'S INVESTIGATE SCIENCE
SCIENCE
Transportation

LET'S INVESTIGATE SCIENCE
SCIENCE
Transportation

Robin Kerrod

Illustrated by Ted Evans

MARSHALL CAVENDISH
NEW YORK · LONDON · TORONTO · SYDNEY

Library Edition Published 1994

© Marshall Cavendish Corporation 1994

Published by Marshall Cavendish Corporation
2415 Jerusalem Avenue
PO Box 587
North Bellmore
New York 11710

Series created by Graham Beehag Book Design

Library of Congress Cataloging-in-Publication Data

Kerrod, Robin.
   Transportation / Robin Kerrod; llustrated by Ted Evans.
   p. cm. -- (Let's investigate science)
   Includes bibliographical references and index.
   ISBN 1-85435-629-1   ISBN 1-85435-688-7 (set)
   1. Transportation--Juvenile literature. [1. Transportation.]
   I. Evans, Ted ill. II. Title. III. Series: Kerrod, Robin.
   Let's investigate science.
   TA1149.K48 1994   93-48726
   629.04--dc20   CIP
                                                             AC

Printed and bound in Hong Kong.

Contents

Introduction   7
For sports and leisure   8

Chapter 1

By Road and Rail   11
The car develops   12
Car anatomy   14
Car engines   16
Systems galore   18
Trucks   20
Motorcycles   22
The locomotive develops   24
The iron road   26
Railroads with a difference   28

Chapter 2

By Air   31
The airplane develops   32
Flying high   34
Principles of flight   36
Controlling flight   38
Out of the ordinary   40
Helicopters and jump jets   42

Chapter 3

By Sea   45
The ship develops   46
On the high seas   48
Basic principles   50
Surface skimmers   52
Under the sea   54

Milestones   56
Glossary   57
Answers   60
For further reading   62
Index   63

Introduction

Our modern way of life depends heavily on transportation by land, sea and air – that is, by car, truck, train, ship, and plane. Our main means of getting around on land, the car, provides us with convenient personal transportation in speed and comfort. And trucks working around the clock and across the country transport every conceivable kind of freight – fuel and other raw materials, manufactured goods, farm produce, and so forth.

Railroad trains no longer carry as many passengers as they once did, but they are a very efficient way of transporting freight in bulk overland. Ships, too, mostly transport freight nationwide and from country to country.

Aircraft beat all other means of transportation for speed. They carry cargo and transport passengers. It is often said that they have made the world a smaller place. Certainly they have revolutionized long-distance travel. At the beginning of the century, a businessperson might take up to a week to cross the Atlantic in an ocean liner. The supersonic airliner Concorde can now whisk him or her across in just three hours!

In this book we look at the main forms of land, air, and sea transportation and on the scientific principles behind them.

You can check your answers to the questions featured throughout this book on pages 60-61.

◀ The supersonic airliner Concorde, pictured above the city of Rio de Janeiro in Brazil. Soon it will be traveling at over 20 miles (32 km) a minute. On the streets of the city, drivers are lucky if they can travel the same distance in an hour!

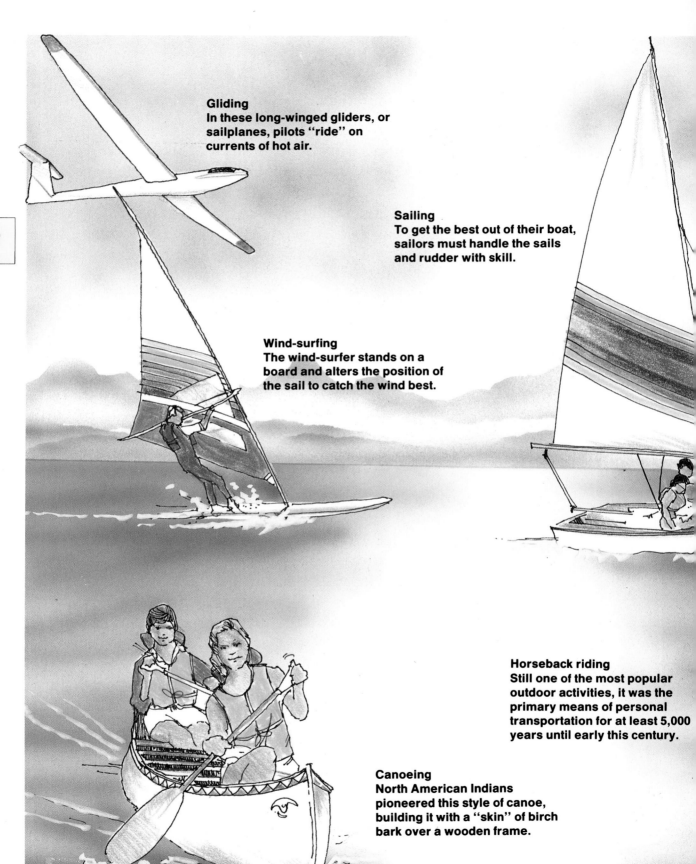

Gliding
In these long-winged gliders, or sailplanes, pilots "ride" on currents of hot air.

Sailing
To get the best out of their boat, sailors must handle the sails and rudder with skill.

Wind-surfing
The wind-surfer stands on a board and alters the position of the sail to catch the wind best.

Horseback riding
Still one of the most popular outdoor activities, it was the primary means of personal transportation for at least 5,000 years until early this century.

Canoeing
North American Indians pioneered this style of canoe, building it with a "skin" of birch bark over a wooden frame.

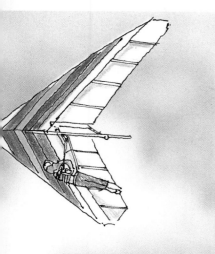

Hang-gliding
The pilot hangs in a harness
underneath a triangular wing.

For sports and leisure

This book concentrates on transportation by machines powered by engines. But we must not forget that there are other means of transportation that rely on what we might call natural power.

Such natural power includes the muscle power of animals – and ourselves – and the power blowing in the wind. Mostly these days we use these natural forms of transportation for sports and leisure. The pictures show a selection of them.

Our early ancestors relied on their legs for transportation. Only after they started to domesticate animals, about 8,000 years ago, did they begin to use animals to ride on and to carry burdens. At about the same time, they began to use rivers for transportation, paddling in canoes that were made by hollowing out tree trunks. Later they discovered that they could harness the wind by hoisting a sail on their boats.

By then, about 5,000 years ago, people had invented the wheel, one of the most important devices in human history. Animal-drawn wheeled carts and coaches remained the prime means of land transportation until steam-engined vehicles began to appear on the roads in the late 1700s and shortly afterward on the railroads.

At the same time people began taking to the air in lighter-than-air balloons and investigating the principles of heavier-than-air flight with gliders. Both ballooning and gliding remain popular leisure activities, hang gliding probably being the closest humans will ever come to flying like a bird.

9

1 By Road and Rail

◄ **Multilane freeways criss-cross the city of Los Angeles, providing rapid transportation most of the time between the suburbs and the center. There are so many vehicles on the highways, however, that the city suffers badly from air pollution.**

▼ **Railroads of a sort existed in mines long before the age of steam. In a typical operation, the wagons would roll downhill under gravity and be pulled back uphill by a horse. This kind of track was often called a tramway.**

Invented only about a century ago, the automobile, or car, has become a dominant feature in most of our lives. It often affects where we live and work, how we organize and spend our leisure time and vacations, and so forth.

Cars are the most numerous of the motor vehicles that travel on our roads, along with trucks and other commercial vehicles, buses, and motorcycles. In the U.S. about 200 million vehicles travel on the nation's 3 ½ million miles (5.6 million km) of paved roads. Millions of new vehicles are pouring onto the roads each year, causing increasing traffic congestion, especially in cities.

In many cities and suburbs people are switching back to railroads for speedier travel, especially to subways, or underground railroads, that are now being built in many cities. Railroads in general have been hard hit over the years by competition from the car and buses for carrying passengers and the truck for carrying freight. But as roads get more congested, railroads will offer an increasingly attractive alternative to road transportation.

▲ The Assyrians and Egyptians in the Middle East began using a swift, horsedrawn chariot afterabout 2000 BC. With a light body, two wheels, and drawn by a pair of horses, it completely changed the art of warfare.

▲ The horse-drawn stagecoach came into use in Europe in the 1600s. It was so called because it ran regularly on a fixed route between a number of stations, or staging posts, where the horses were usually changed.

The car develops

Passenger road traffic was pioneered by the stagecoach in the 1600s and became increasingly important over the next 200 years. In the early 1800s improved coach design and the building of better-surfaced roads led to an upsurge in passenger traffic. But by the 1840s the newly built railroads had killed off the stagecoach, except in remote areas, such as the American West.

While some engineers built steam locomotives for the railroads, others experimented with steam-powered road vehicles. Passenger-carrying steam carriages enjoyed brief popularity in the 1830s. Light steam cars for personal use were more successful, and many thousands were built in the U.S. Best known were the Stanley Steamers, built by the Stanley brothers from 1897. By then, electric-powered cars were also becoming popular.

But a new type of car had also appeared on the scene and was destined to make steamers and electric cars obsolete.

The gasoline revolution

It was two German engineers, Gottlieb Daimler and Karl Benz, who ushered in a new era in motoring with their gasoline-engined vehicles. Independently, in 1885, they built lightweight gasoline engines. Daimler first fitted one in a bicycle frame to create the first motor cycle. Benz designed a totally new vehicle around his engine to create the ancestor of the modern car.

Daimler fitted one of his engines into a horse carriage in 1886 to create the first four-wheeled motor car. For many years this new means of transportation was termed the horseless carriage.

In Europe and the United States the car developed rapidly. The Duryea brothers, Charles and James, built the first U.S. car in 1893. Henry Ford built his first car in 1896, as did Ransome Olds, and "Ford" and "Oldsmobile" would become two of the most famous names in car history.

It was in 1908 that Ford ushered in the age of the modern car by streamlining production on an assembly line. He also concentrated on one design, the Model T, nicknamed the "Tin Lizzie" because the body was built with thin (but strong) sheet steel. In 1913 Ford increased production further by introducing moving conveyors onto the production line. The price of the Model T eventually fell as low as $260. By 1927 over 15 million had been sold.

▼ Karl Benz's three-wheeler of 1885, the first practical motor car. It was designed from scratch as a motor vehicle, and was not, like Daimler's machine, a horse carriage with an engine.

▲ Nicolas Cugnot's second steam tractor of 1770, which still exists in a Paris museum.

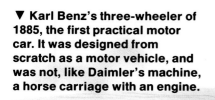

◄ Ransome E. Olds's "curved dash" Oldsmobile of 1901 was built on an assembly line.

13

◄ Henry Ford's famous Model T, introduced in 1908. By using mass-production techniques and concentrating on this one model, Ford was able to produce it cheaply, bringing motoring within the reach of ordinary people.

► Another Ford legend, the famous Ford V-8 of the 1930s, so-called because its cylinders were arranged in a V-shape.

◄ The 1940s and 1950s were decades of big, heavy cars with "thirsty" engines, which consumed large amounts of gasoline. They were often called "gas-guzzlers." No attempts were made to streamline the bodies.

Car anatomy

Most people, when they are old enough, find it relatively easy to drive a car. The modern car is very "user-friendly." But this belies the fact that it is a very complex machine. It is made up of thousands of different components, from tiny steel ball bearings a fraction of an inch across to the heavy cast-iron block that forms the engine.

14

Q 1. On the average, how many components do you think there are in a car: **(A)** 2,500, **(B)** 5,000, **(C)** 8,500, **(D)** 11,000, **(E)** 12,500, or **(F)** 14,000?

Being systematic

To understand how a car works, it is best to think of it as made up of a number of separate units, or systems. Each system plays its part in making the car go. Major systems include the body, the engine, and the transmission.

Outwardly, the shape of a car changes year by year as new models are introduced. In general, cars are much sleeker looking than they once were, with smooth, flowing lines. They are becoming more streamlined so that they "slip" through the air with the least resistance, or drag. To this end, new designs are tested in wind tunnels, just like aircraft.

There are two main methods of building a car body. Once all U.S. cars had a body made of sheet steel built on a separate reinforced framework, or chassis. This method is still used for larger cars. But most cars have a body designed as a single unit, or shell, following the practice in most other countries. The body shell is constructed of welded steel panels, which together provide the necessary strength and stiffness. It is much lighter than chassis construction and lends itself better to automated production.

Q 2. What do you think is the main advantage in streamlining a car?

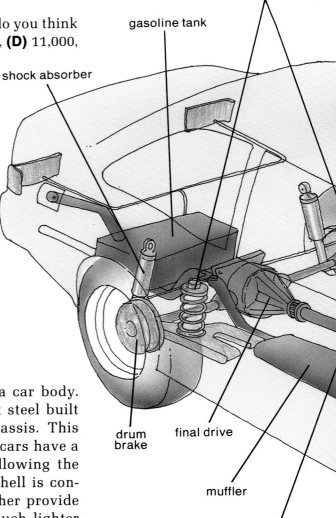

rear suspension

gasoline tank

shock absorber

drum brake

final drive

muffler

propeller shaft

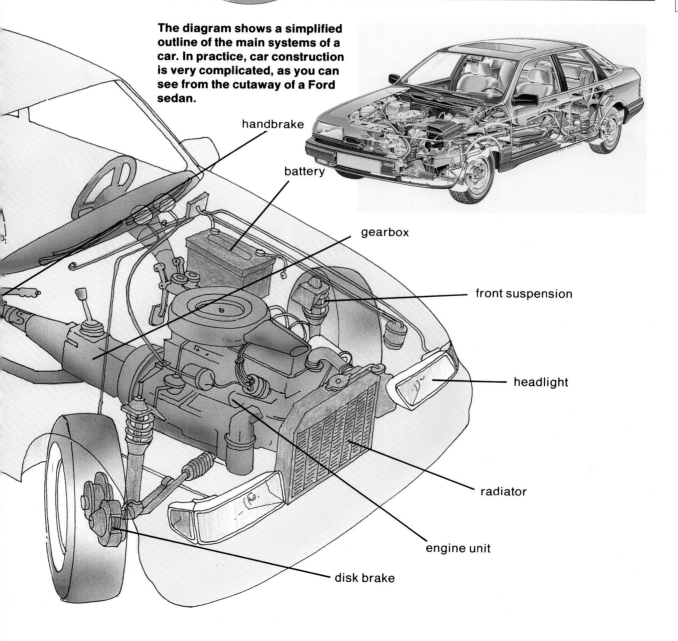

WORKOUT

The pie chart (left) shows the proportion of motor vehicles in the U.S. that are cars. From the chart and using the data given in the text on page 11, figure out how many cars there are on U.S. roads. If on the average a car is 13 feet (4 meters) long, how many cars are there per mile (per kilometer) of road in the U.S.?

cars

other vehicles

The diagram shows a simplified outline of the main systems of a car. In practice, car construction is very complicated, as you can see from the cutaway of a Ford sedan.

handbrake

battery

gearbox

front suspension

headlight

radiator

engine unit

disk brake

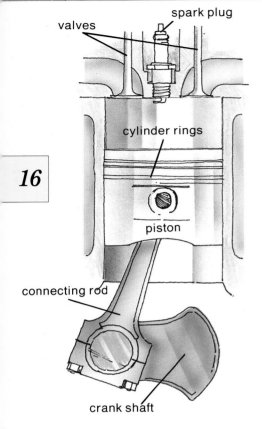

valves

spark plug

cylinder rings

piston

connecting rod

crank shaft

◀ **A piston and cylinder. The piston rings insure a tight fit. Valves at the top of the cylinder allow fuel mixture in and exhaust gases out. The spark plug produces an electric spark. A connecting rod ("con rod") links the piston and crankshaft.**

▼ **The four-stroke cycle of a gasoline engine – Intake, Compression, Power, and Exhaust – showing the operating sequence of the valves and the movements of the piston. The cycle is repeated over and over in each cylinder as the engine turns.**

Car engines

Most cars are powered by an engine that uses gasoline as fuel. The gasoline engine is the most common type of internal combustion engine. It is a piston engine, in which pistons move up and down inside cylinders. In the engine, gasoline is mixed with air to form an explosive vapor and then introduced into the engine cylinders. There it is exploded by electric sparks. The hot gases produced expand and drive the pistons down the cylinders.

The pistons are connected by connecting rods to a crankshaft. This shaft, which looks a little like a complicated winding handle, converts the up-and-down motion of the connecting rods into rotary motion. At the end on the crankshaft a heavy flywheel passes on the engine power to the car's transmission system, which takes it to the driving wheels.

Q Where does gasoline come from?

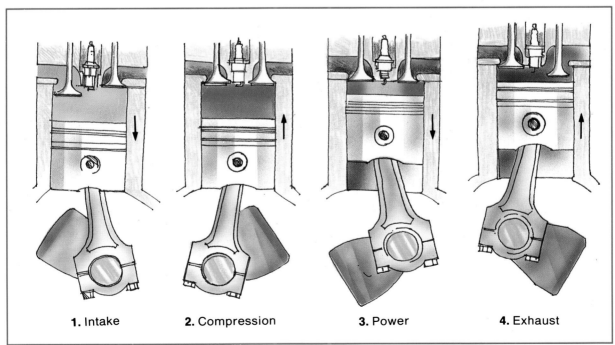

1. Intake **2.** Compression **3.** Power **4.** Exhaust

The engine cycle

To produce power, the engine goes through a repetitive cycle, or a number of movements that are repeated time and time again. It is called the four-stroke cycle because in each engine cylinder power is produced once in every four strokes, or movements, of the piston. The cycle is illustrated on the left.

On the first downward stroke (Intake) of the piston, a mixture of gasoline and air is drawn into the cylinder through the open intake valve. The exhaust valve is closed. The intake valve now opens as the piston moves up on its second stroke (Compression), compressing the fuel mixture.

The spark plug now produces a spark that ignites the mixture. The hot gases that are produced now expand forcing the piston down on its third stroke (Power). As the piston comes up on its fourth stroke (Exhaust), it pushes the burned gases out of the open exhaust valve. The exhaust valve now closes, the intake valve opens, and the piston begins moving down to begin another cycle.

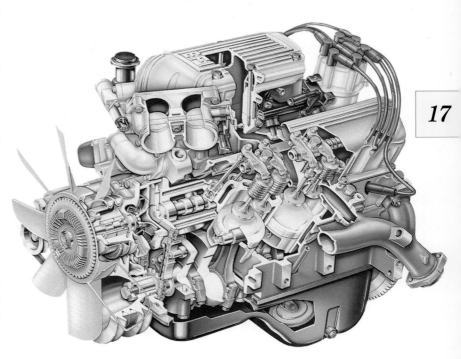

17

▲ **A look inside a car engine, showing the mechanisms needed to keep it working. This engine is called a V-6, which means that its six cylinders are arranged in two banks of three, set at an angle to each other in the shape of a V. Many car engines have all their cylinders in line.**

Drawbacks

One drawback of the gasoline engine is that it is not particularly efficient. It harnesses only about 25 percent of the energy in the gasoline fuel. This is one of the reasons that many people are turning to cars with diesel engines. These engines can harness as much as 40 percent of the energy in their fuel, which is a kind of light oil. But diesel engines are found mostly in commercial vehicles, such as trucks and buses (see page 20), rather than cars.

Q What is another serious drawback of the gasoline engine?

18

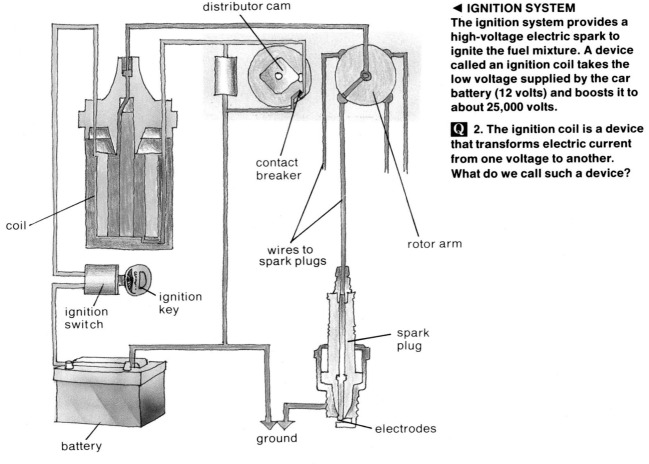

distributor cam

contact
breaker

coil

wires to
spark plugs

rotor arm

ignition switch

ignition key

spark
plug

battery

ground

electrodes

◀ **IGNITION SYSTEM**

The ignition system provides a high-voltage electric spark to ignite the fuel mixture. A device called an ignition coil takes the low voltage supplied by the car battery (12 volts) and boosts it to about 25,000 volts.

Q 2. The ignition coil is a device that transforms electric current from one voltage to another. What do we call such a device?

▶ **COOLING SYSTEM**

The cooling system removes excess heat from the engine. The gasoline mixture burns in the cylinders at a temperature of more than 1,300°F (700°C). If the heat were not removed, the engine would rapidly overheat. Almost all car engines are water-cooled. Water gets hot as it circulates through passages in the engine block. The water rises through the engine as it is heated and passes into the top of the radiator. It then drops down through the radiator tubes and is cooled by air flowing past them. A water pump helps the natural circulation.

Q 1. What do we call the natural circulation in water that is being heated?

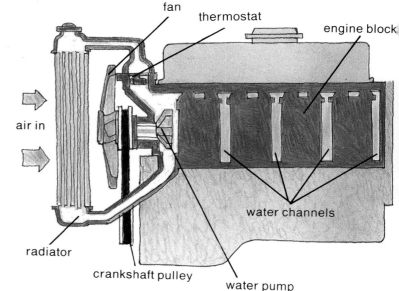

fan

thermostat

engine block

air in

water channels

radiator

crankshaft pulley

water pump

► **BRAKING SYSTEM**
This slows down or stops the car by forcing pads or linings against a disk or drum attached to each wheel. In fact, cars have two independent braking systems. The hand-operated parking brake works mechanically and usually acts only on the rear wheels. The main braking system is operated by the brake pedal and acts on all four wheels. It is a hydraulic (liquid) pressure system. Pressing the brake pedal forces liquid through pipes to each wheel, where it pushes against a piston that applies the brakes.

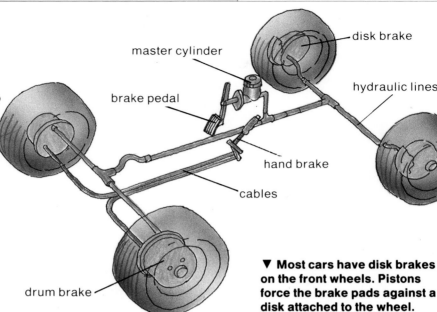

master cylinder

brake pedal

disk brake

hydraulic lines

hand brake

cables

drum brake

19

▼ **Most cars have disk brakes on the front wheels. Pistons force the brake pads against a disk attached to the wheel.**

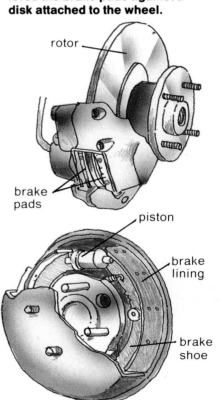

rotor

brake pads

piston

brake lining

brake shoe

▲ **Many cars have drum brakes like this on the rear wheels. Pistons force the brake linings against a drum attached to the wheel.**

Systems galore

As mentioned earlier, a car is a collection of systems that work together. We have room here to describe only a few of them. You can find out more about other systems by looking at entries in the Glossary indicated in CAPITAL letters below.

The engine is made up of a number of systems. The fuel system delivers fuel into the engine. This may be done through a carburetor or by fuel injection.

The ignition system (opposite top) provides the spark to ignite the fuel mixture. The cooling system (opposite bottom) removes excess heat from the engine. The LUBRICATION system keeps the engine oiled.

The transmission is the other major car system involved in delivering power. The transmission of a car with rear-wheel drive consists of CLUTCH, GEARBOX, PROPELLER SHAFT, and FINAL DRIVE. The transmission of a front-wheel drive car has no propeller shaft. The clutch, gearbox, and final drive are directly linked to the engine unit. Four-wheel drive cars have the engine driving both front and rear wheels.

Other essential systems in a car include BRAKING (see above), STEERING, and SUSPENSION.

Q Why is it necessary to oil an engine? What happens if an engine runs out of oil?

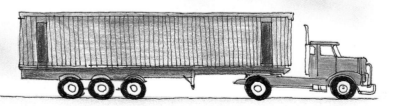

20

Trucks

As the pictures on these pages show, trucks come in all shapes and sizes. As freight carriers, they carry almost every kind of load you can think of – milk and mail, cars and concrete, lumber and live-stock, and so forth – all across the nation. And when mounted with different bodies, they can also, for example, become fire engines or mobile cranes.

There are two main kinds of trucks – straight and trac-tor-trailers. A straight truck is constructed with a single frame, or chassis, and two or more axles. Different bodies can be mounted on the chassis.

Tractor-trailer trucks consist of two units, joined by a flexible coupling, usually called the "fifth wheel." The two units are a truck tractor and a semitrailer. The tractor is an engine-and-cab unit with a short chassis, which carries the coupling. This slides into a coupling on the underside of the semitrailer.

Truck systems

Some trucks have a gasoline engine like a car, but large trucks have diesel engines. The diesel en-

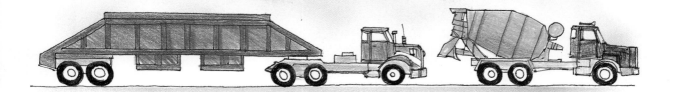

gine uses a light oil as fuel. The engine is built in much the same way as a gasoline engine. One notable exception is that it does not have any spark plugs.

The fuel mixture in the engine cylinders is ignited by compression. Compressing the air in the cylinders makes it heat up. When diesel fuel is injected into the hot air, it immediately burns.

To haul heavy loads under different road conditions, trucks need more gears than cars. Most large trucks have two gearboxes that give them a total of ten or more gears.

Heavy trucks also need stronger brakes than cars do. Usually they have air brakes, in which the brakes are applied against the wheels by compressed air. The compressed air is supplied by an engine-driven compressor, or pump. The air is stored in tanks and released when the driver applies the brakes.

Q **(A)** Heavy trucks usually have three or more axles. The rear ones often have two wheels each side. Why is this a good idea? **(B)** What are the advantages of a tractor-trailer?

WORKOUT

This pie chart shows the proportion of motor vehicles in the U.S. that are trucks. From the chart and using the data given in the text on page 11, calculate how many trucks there are on U.S. roads.

If on the average a truck is 40 feet (12 meters) long, how many trucks are there per mile (per kilometer) of road in the U.S.?

trucks

other vehicles

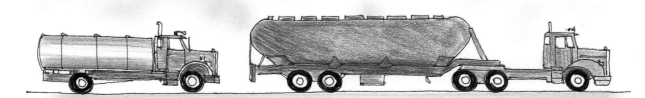

Motorcycles

The first motorcycle took to the streets as early as 1868. It was a steam-powered machine, built by the French brothers Pierre and Ernest Michaux. Gottlieb Daimler in Germany built the first gasoline-engined motorcycle in 1885, before turning his attention to building "horseless carriages" (see page 12).

22

The modern motorcycle combines features of the bicycle and the car. Like a bike, it has a front wheel mounted in a fork, which is turned by handlebars for steering. In most motorcycles, the rear wheel is driven by a chain.

Most motorcycles are powered by a gasoline engine that works on the four-stroke cycle (see page 16). It is built in much the same way as a car engine, but is more compact. It usually has only one or two cylinders. Many small motorcycles have two-stroke engines, which produce power on every downward stroke (movement) of the piston. Two-stroke engines are simpler and easier to care for than are four-stroke engines.

A motorcycle has many of the same kind of systems as a car — ignition, fuel, lubrication, cooling, transmission, and so forth. The ignition, fuel, and lubrication systems are similar to those of a car. Most bikes have an air-cooling system and chain drive. Some larger machines have water cooling, similar to that of a car, and have their rear wheel driven by a shaft from the engine. Like a car, motorcycles have a clutch and gearbox for changing gears.

The rider controls the bike with both hands and both feet. The left hand operates the clutch lever; the left foot, the gear-shift pedal. The right hand operates both the twist-grip throttle to control engine speed and the front-brake lever. The right foot operates the rear-brake pedal.

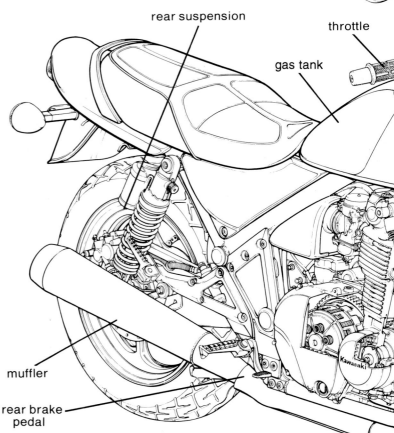

rear suspension

throttle

gas tank

muffler

rear brake pedal

exhaust pipes

▲ **The main features of a modern motorcycle. This kind of bike gives a breathtaking performance. It can accelerate from 0 to 60 mph (100 km/h) in a few seconds.**

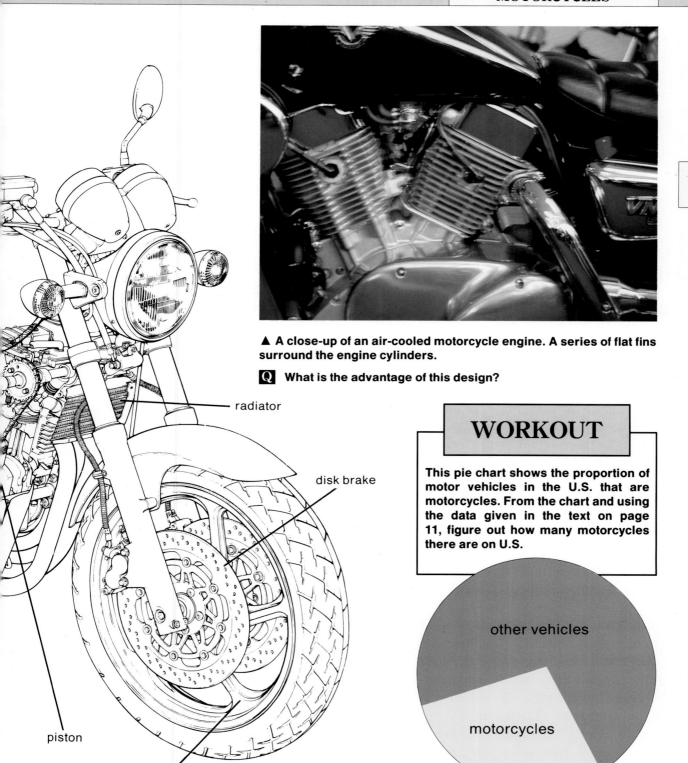

▲ **A close-up of an air-cooled motorcycle engine. A series of flat fins surround the engine cylinders.**

Q **What is the advantage of this design?**

radiator

disk brake

piston

alloy wheel

WORKOUT

This pie chart shows the proportion of motor vehicles in the U.S. that are motorcycles. From the chart and using the data given in the text on page 11, figure out how many motorcycles there are on U.S.

other vehicles

motorcycles

The locomotive develops

A British engineer named Richard Trevithick began experimenting with steam-powered vehicles in the early 1800s. He tried running them on the roads, but with little success. So he decided to run them instead on a prepared "road" of iron rails — a railroad track, beginning in 1804.

Soon other British engineers started building locomotives. Outstanding among them was George Stephenson, who went on to build and equip the first public railroads to be operated by steam — the Stockton and Darlington line (1825) and the Liverpool and Manchester (1830). With the opening of the latter, the Age of the Railroad began.

Opening up America

The potential of the railroad for transportation across the vast open spaces of the U.S. was quickly appreciated. An engineer named John Stevens, at a sprightly 76 years old, ran the first experimental steam locomotive in the country in 1825. Four years later a locomotive imported from Britain, the *Stourbridge Lion*, ran briefly on a track of the Delaware and Hudson Canal Company.

But it was the first American-built locomotive, *Best Friend* of Charleston, that inaugurated the nation's first passenger service, on the South Carolina Railroad, on Christmas Day in 1830. Within ten years the U.S. had more than 3,000 miles (5,000 km) of track. By 1860 there were 30,000 miles (50,000 km) of track.

In 1863 work started on the first transcontinental railroad, with construction teams working toward each other from opposite sides of the continent. One began driving east from Sacramento, California; the other drove west from Omaha, Nebraska. They met at Promontory, Utah, in May 1869. The completion of this 1,725-mile (2,775-km) line provided the springboard for the settlement of previously inaccessible parts of the country.

Steam locomotives dominated the railroads until the 1940s, reaching their pinnacle in the aptly named Big Boys. But in a little over ten years they had all but disappeared, being replaced by the much cleaner and more efficient diesels.

Almost all of today's U.S. locomotives are diesels. In other countries electric locomotives are widely used. They power the fastest modern trains, like the famous Japanese "bullet trains," for example.

► ►

1. Richard Trevithick's pioneering locomotive *New Castle*. He ran it on the tramway at an iron mine in southern Wales in February 1804. It hauled a train with five wagons, loaded with 10 tons of iron ore and 70 passengers.

2. George Stephenson's locomotive *Rocket*, with which he opened the Liverpool and Manchester line in 1830. It was the first locomotive to use the more efficient multitube boiler, a feature of all steam locomotives from then on.

3. The *John Bull*, built by George Stephenson's son Robert, was purchased for the Camden and Ambroy Railroad in the U.S. in 1831.

4. The *De Witt Clinton* opened the Mohawk and Hudson Railroad in 1831. Passengers sitting in open wagons behind the locomotive spent much of the time putting out fires started by sparks and cinders from the chimney!

5. An American standard locomotive of the 1860s. More than 20,000 of this design were built. It featured a prominent cowcatcher and enormous chimney. This was designed to prevent the escape of sparks.

6. The streamlined *Mallard*, the British steam locomotive that achieved a record speed (for steam) of 126 mph (202 km/h) in 1938. The record still stands.

7. Distinctive streamlined steam locomotives like this hauled passenger trains in the U.S. during the 1940s. Called streamliners, they were the "bullet trains" of the steam era.

8. Big Boy, one of the biggest and most powerful steam locomotives ever built. Weighing some 600 tons (550 tonnes), it had the pulling power of 6,000 horses. They were used for hauling freight in the 1940s and 1950s.

1.

2.

3.

4.

5.

6.

7.

8.

The iron road

The railroad has often been called the "iron road," for this is in fact what it is. The French name for the railroad, chemin de fer, literally means "road of iron." The standard railroad track consists of twin rails with a flat bottom, called T-rails, because of their shape.

The rails rest in tieplates (baseplates), which are fixed to crossties at right angles to the track. The crossties themselves are set firmly in a ballast of crushed rock. The crossties may be wooden or concrete. The standard length of rail in the U.S. is 39 feet (nearly 12 meters). But these days many rails are welded together to form continuous lengths sometimes miles long. This eliminates the regular "clickety-click" noise of the wheels running over the joints between standard-length rails.

March of the railroad

So important was the railroad in promoting European settlement of the United States that it is often said "America built the railroads, but the railroads built America." And the U.S. still has the most extensive railroad system in the world. The total mileage is now about 222,000 miles (360,000 km), down from a peak of nearly 270,000 miles (430,000 km) early this century. Nearly all the track is standard gauge – the width between the rails, of 4 feet 8 ½ inches (143.5 cm).

U.S. railroads are operated by literally hundreds of different companies. But long-distance intercity passenger services are operated nationwide by a single company, Amtrak, the National Railroad Passenger Corporation. Amtrak provides services over some 40,000 miles (64,000 km) of route and carries over 20 million passengers a year.

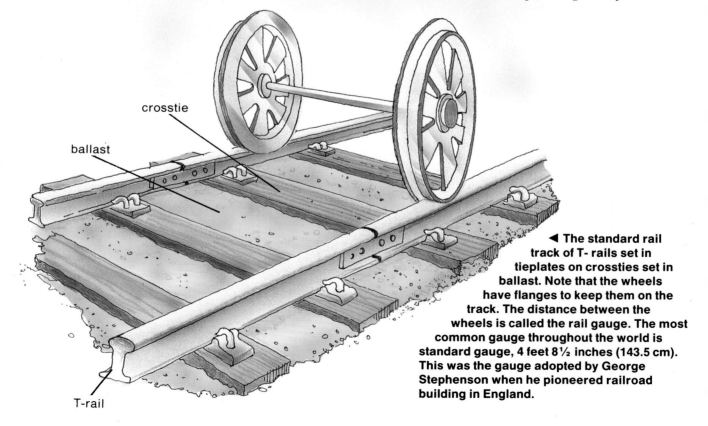

crosstie

ballast

T-rail

◀ The standard rail track of T- rails set in tieplates on crossties set in ballast. Note that the wheels have flanges to keep them on the track. The distance between the wheels is called the rail gauge. The most common gauge throughout the world is standard gauge, 4 feet 8½ inches (143.5 cm). This was the gauge adopted by George Stephenson when he pioneered railroad building in England.

▲ An Amtrak diesel-powered train. Most American trains are pulled by locomotives powered by diesel engines. They have diesel-electric drive. The diesel engine drives a generator, which produces electricity to spin electric motors that turn the wheels.

▶ This Amtrak "Turboliner" is so-called because it has a gas-turbine locomotive. The turbine is used to spin a generator to produce electricity, which is fed to motors that drive the wheels.

▶ This Amtrak locomotive picks up electric current from overhead power lines with a sprung arm called a pantograph. It operates at a voltage of about 25,000 volts.

Railroads with a difference

On most railroads, the locomotives have smooth steel wheels and run on smooth steel track. The track has to be more or less level, otherwise the wheels may start to slip. Yet on some mountain railroads the locomotives are able to climb slopes with a gradient (slope) of 1 in 2. This means that for every two feet traveled forward, they climb 1 foot upward!

Most of these steep mountain railroads are operated by a rack-and-pinion system. The track includes an extra rail with slots or teeth cut in it (the rack), and the locomotive carries a toothed wheel (the pinion). The teeth of the pinion engage with the slots or teeth of the rack, thus preventing slippage. The first rack mountain railroad was built on Mount Washington, New Hampshire, in 1869. It is still in use today.

The rack railroad is one of a number of different kinds of railroad systems that operate in different parts of the world. The pictures on these pages show some of the others, including cable-hauled systems, subways, monorails, and maglevs. The maglev (magnetically levitated) train is one of the most exciting recent developments in land transportation. It could make possible speeds as high as 500 mph (800 km/h)!

28

THE BIG APPLE SUBWAY

The New York Subway, opened in 1904, is one of the biggest subway systems in the world. About 1 billion passengers travel on its 232 miles (373 km) of track and pass through its 466 stations every year.

Q How many people on the average pass through a station every day?

◄ An experimental maglev vehicle at speed. It is elevated above the track by magnetic repulsion – a magnet on the train pushes against the magnetism of the track. The track is a monorail (single-rail).

► A car on the Mt. Pilatus rack railroad in Switzerland. It is the steepest railroad in the world. It began operation in 1889.

▼ San Francisco's unique form of rail transportation, the cablecar. Inventor Andrew Hallidie introduced the cablecar in 1873. It is hauled by moving cables running underneath the streets.

2
By Air

◄ A trio of jet planes streaks through the sky. It is the jet engine that makes it possible for aircraft to travel so fast.

Traveling by airplane is the most recent of our major forms of transportation. While air travel is less than a century old, today major airports handle hundreds of planes and hundreds of thousands of passengers every day. Chicago's O'Hare Airport is one of the busiest in the world, handling close to 60 million passengers a year.

Airplanes, usually just called planes, are the most common kind of flying machines, or aircraft. But they are not the only kind. Balloons, airships, or blimps, and helicopters are others. Helicopters are perhaps the perfect flying machine, able to take off and land in a small space, fly in any direction, and hover in the air like a humming bird.

Air travel is by far the fastest means of transportation. An ordinary airliner can cruise at a speed of over 500 mph (800 km/h) – a speed that is five times faster than most trains. Some airforce combat planes can travel much faster.

Q The fastest combat planes can travel at speeds up to 2,200 mph (3,500 km/h). If you flew in such a plane at such a speed, how far would you travel between your heart beats?

(☆ **Hint:** Time how long it takes your heart to beat – 30 beats, then divide by 30.)

◄ With spectators looking on in astonishment, an elaborately decorated hot-air balloon made by the Montgolfier brothers takes off from Annonay, near Lyons, in southern France, in 1783. This flight marked the beginning of aviation.

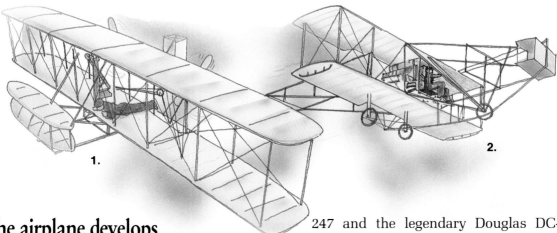

The airplane develops

Humans first took to the air in balloons. The Montgolfier brothers in France built the first balloons, filled with hot air, in 1783. Other people built balloons filled with hydrogen gas. Later, they fitted engines to balloons to create airships.

Q **1.** How do balloons filled with hot air or hydrogen stay up in the air?

The Wrights get it right

The story of air transportation really began, however, with the Wright brothers. They made the first airplane flight, in *Flyer*, on December 17, 1903.

The first flight lasted only 12 seconds and took *Flyer* only about 120 feet (37 meters), but it showed the way ahead.

Q **2.** What was *Flyer*'s average speed? Give your answer in mph (km/h).

Rise of the monoplanes

Flyer and most other early planes were biplanes, with two wings. In 1909 French aviator Louis Bleriot pioneered the single-wing craft, or monoplane. But it was not until the 1930s that monoplanes began to dominate the skies. That was the time of famous international air races

Passenger air travel at the time was only just beginning. But in the mid-1930s the introduction of new sleek all-metal planes such as the Boeing 247 and the legendary Douglas DC-3 *Dakota* made air travel much more comfortable and safer.

The jet age

The airplane developed rapidly during World War II, and by the war's end a revolutionary new kind of plane had appeared – the jet. This plane used a jet of hot gases rather than a rotating propeller for propulsion. Jets were used first by the military, but in the 1950s the first jet airliners, such as the British De Havilland *Comet* and the Boeing 707, appeared and pioneered the modern age of air travel.

1. The Wright brothers' *Flyer*, in which they pioneered airplane flight in 1903.

2. Glenn Curtiss's *Golden Flyer* of 1909. Curtiss became one of the top U.S. aviators in the early days of flying.

3. Louis Bleriot's pioneering monoplane, in which he made the first flight across the English Channel in July 1909. The 31-mile (50-km) crossing took just 37 minutes.

4. The Curtiss *Jenny* biplane was built by the thousands as a trainer for pilots during World War 1 and was widely used for "barnstorming" afterward.

5. The British Supermarine S6B float plane was built to compete in international air races.

6. The Douglas DC-3 *Dakota* first flew in December 1935, more than 10,000 were manufactured.

7. The Lockheed *Constellation* was one of the long-range four-engined aircraft that helped spur the development of civil aviation after World War II.

8. The Bell X-1 rocket plane, in which Chuck Yeager became the first person to break through the "sound barrier" and fly faster than the speed of sound in 1947.

9. The Boeing 747, which made its first flight in February 1969 and pioneered the era of "jumbo jet" travel. With its wide 196-feet (60-meter) body, it could carry more than 400 passengers.

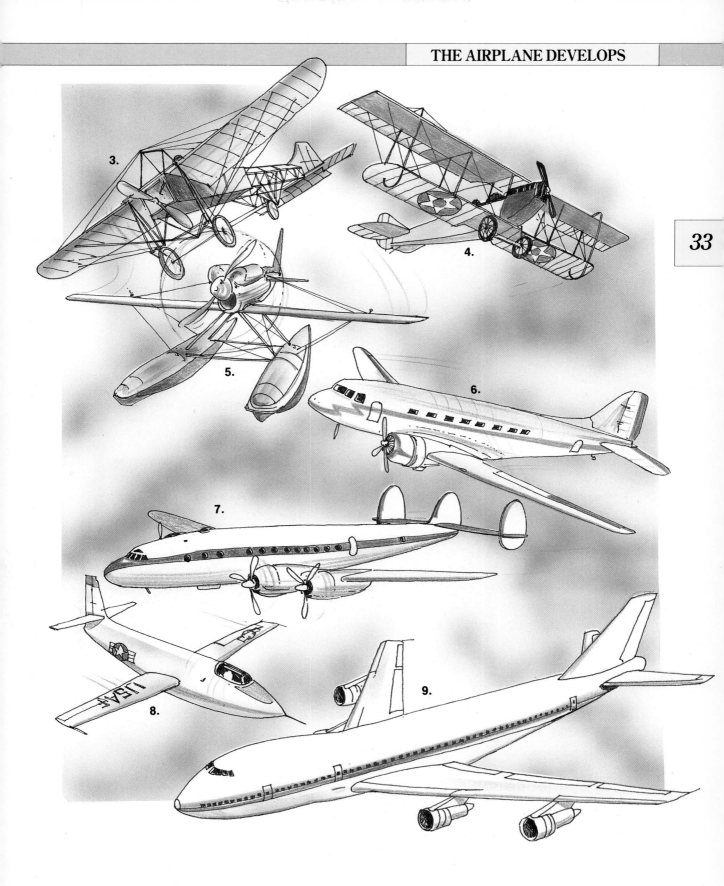

3.

4.

5.

6.

7.

8.

9.

34

Flying high

Billions of passengers now travel on the world's airlines every year, nearly half a billion in the United States alone. The U.S. has one of the world's most developed airline systems, with routes connecting all major cities. Large airports such as Hartsfield Atlanta International Airport and Chicago's O'Hare International Airport handle over a million passengers a week. In the private sector, several hundred thousand people hold pilot's licenses and fly regularly.

As a visit to your local airport will show, a variety of planes come and go, from single-engined private airplanes propelled by propeller to wide-bodied "jumbo jets" carrying hundreds of passengers.

▲ The Lockheed Tristar is a long-range wide-bodied airliner, able to seat up to 400 passengers. With one engine in the tail and one slung under each wing, it is slightly smaller than the DC-10, which has the same engine arrangement.

◄ The Boeing 727 is one of the most successful medium-range airliners. Its three engines are located at the rear, one in the tail and one on each side of the fuselage.

Planes differ widely not only in size but also in design, as the pictures on this page show. Small private planes and transport planes, which cruise at relatively low speeds, have their wings projecting more or less at right-angles to the fuselage (body). But most airliners have swept-back wings, which allows them to cruise at much higher speeds.

Planes also vary in the number and positions of their engines. The Boeing 747 has four engines, slung beneath the wings. The Douglas DC-10 has three engines, one under each wing and one in the tail. The Boeing 767 has one engine under each wing.

The Boeing 747 is one of the most distinctive planes in the skies, not only because of its size but also because of its bulbous front fuselage. This accommodates an upper deck level, which is usually set up as a first-class lounge.

The original jumbo jet, the Boeing 747, first took to the skies in 1969. It still dominates long-distance national and intercontinental routes. One of the longest routes it flies is from Los Angeles to Sydney, Australia, a distance of some 7,500 miles (12,000 kilometers).

Q A Boeing 747 cruises at an average speed of 500 mph (800 km/h). How long would it take to fly non-stop from Los Angeles to Sydney?

▲ Light aircraft provide vital transportation in countries with a scattered population. Here, in Australia, "flying doctors" are about to fly a patient to a hospital.

▼ Four engines, two under each wing, power the Boeing 747 jumbo jet. Aptly named, it measures 230 feet (70.5 meters) long and has a wingspan of nearly 196 feet (60 meters). It could in theory carry over 500 economy-class passengers.

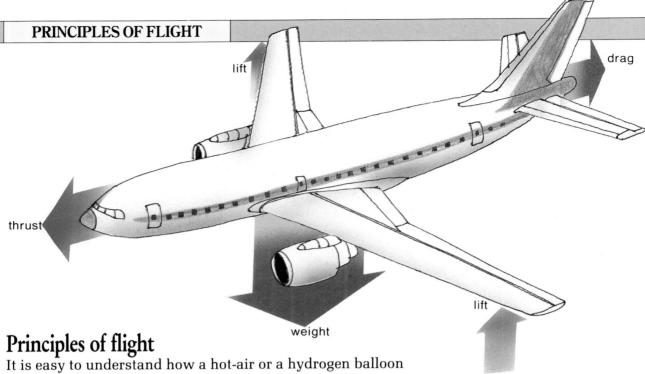

lift

drag

thrust

weight

lift

Principles of flight

It is easy to understand how a hot-air or a hydrogen balloon can lift off the ground and fly. They do so because they are lighter than air. But how can a huge aircraft like the Boeing 747 jumbo jet lift off the ground and fly? Fully loaded, it tips the scales at more than 380 tons (350 tonnes)!

The jumbo jet and other airplanes gain the lift they need to support themselves in the air from their wings, and particularly from the shape of the wings. The wings are flat underneath and curved on top; they are broad at the front and taper sharply at the rear. This kind of shape is called an airfoil.

When air flows past an airfoil or an airfoil travels through the air, the air above it travels faster than that the air underneath (see diagram, right). But as air travels faster, its pressure drops. This means that the pressure above an airfoil is lower than the pressure underneath. This sets up an upward force on it that we call lift. The faster the airfoil moves, the greater the lift it experiences.

Q Relate the principle of the airfoil to airplane flight and explain how a heavy plane can get off the ground.

Plane propulsion

In the early days of flying, all airplanes were propelled by propellers spun

▲ The four main forces that act on a plane in flight. The plane's weight acts downward. The lift provided by the wings acts upward. The thrust provided by the engines acts forward. And the air resistance, or drag, acts backward.

▼ This diagram shows the shape of an airfoil and the kind of air flow around it. Because the upper surface is curved, the air traveling over it has farther to go to reach the rear at the same time as air flowing underneath. It therefore travels faster.

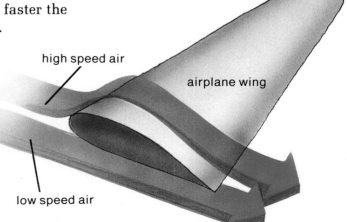

high speed air

airplane wing

low speed air

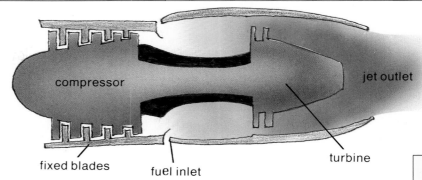

around by gasoline engines. A propeller has a special twisted shape and, in effect, "screws" itself through the air. ("Airscrew" is another name for it.)

Most planes today, however, are propelled by jet engines. A jet engine burns a petroleum fuel called kerosene to produce hot gases. The gases shoot backward out of the engine at high speed, and this sets up a force in the opposite direction that propels the engine forward. The forward force is called thrust.

There are two main kinds of jet engine, the turbojet and the turbofan (see diagrams, right). Turbofans are fitted to almost all airliners. Another kind of jet engine used for low-speed planes is the turboprop. This has an extra turbine to spin a propeller, which provides much of the engine thrust.

Q The principle of jet propulsion follows from a law of motion first stated by a famous English scientist. Who was he, and what does the law state?

compressor

jet outlet

turbine

fixed blades

fuel inlet

▲ This is the simplest kind of jet engine, the turbojet. The compressor channels air into the combustion chamber, where fuel is sprayed in and burned. The hot gases that are produced spin the turbine as they escape rapidly as a jet.

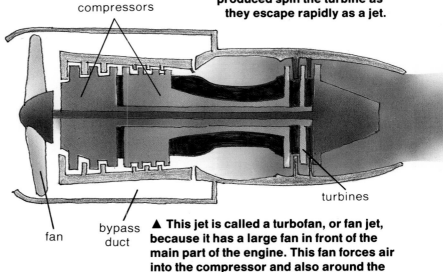

compressors

turbines

fan

bypass duct

▲ This jet is called a turbofan, or fan jet, because it has a large fan in front of the main part of the engine. This fan forces air into the compressor and also around the main part of the engine.

INVESTIGATE

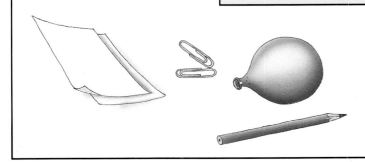

Here are a few things you can use to show some of the principles of flight. What you have to do is: (A) Make an airfoil and demonstrate how it works. (B) Make a flying "machine" with wings. (C) Demonstrate the principle of jet propulsion.

Controlling flight

Like birds, all planes have wings, and they also have a tail. Do they need a tail? Make a paper plane and try flying it without its tail and you will get your answer!

The tail helps to steady, or stabilize, a plane's flight through the air. A plane has a natural tendency to swing left or right, in a movement called yawing. This is corrected by the upright part of the tail, called the tail fin or vertical stabilizer. Another natural movement of a plane is pitching, or moving up and down. This is corrected by the horizontal part of the tail, the tailplane or horizontal stabilizer.

38

The control surfaces

A pilot steers a plane by moving hinged "control surfaces" located at the rear of the wings and tail. They work by deflecting the air flowing past them. The force of the air being deflected in one direction sets up a force in the other that moves the wings or tail in a certain way.

The control surfaces are the ailerons (on the wings), the elevators (on the horizontal stabilizer) and the rudder (on the vertical stabilizer). The pilot operates the ailerons and elevators from a control column (or wheel) in the cockpit. He or she operates the rudder by means of pedals.

Moving the control column from side to side operates the ailerons. Moving them to the left, for example, raises the aileron on the left wing and lowers the one on the right wing.

Moving the control column forward and backward operates the elevators. Pulling on the control column, for example, raises the elevators. Pressing the right rudder pedal moves the rudder to the right.

THINK ABOUT IT

These three diagrams illustrate the movements of a plane's control surfaces mentioned in the text. What effect do these movements have on the attitude, or position, of the plane in the air?

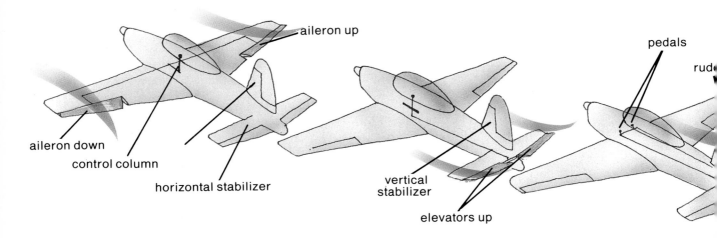

aileron up

pedals

rud

aileron down

control column

horizontal stabilizer

vertical stabilizer

elevators up

▼ This picture illustrates the various control surfaces and other movable surfaces that a pilot operates to control the plane in the air. As you can see, the wings carry several other hinged surfaces besides the ailerons. These flaps, slats, and spoilers come into operation particularly during take-off and landing.

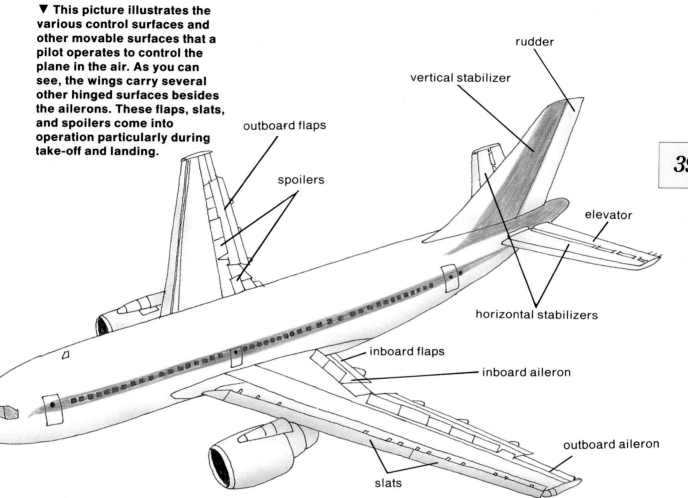

rudder

vertical stabilizer

outboard flaps

spoilers

elevator

horizontal stabilizers

inboard flaps

inboard aileron

outboard aileron

slats

► When an airliner takes off, both the inboard and the outboard flaps are fully extended, as can be seen in the picture. Extending the flaps in effect increases the area and curvature of the wings. This gives the wings increased lift, which is needed when the plane is traveling at low speeds.

40

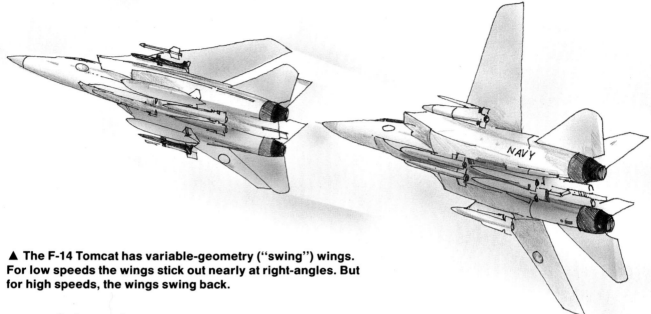

▲ The F-14 Tomcat has variable-geometry ("swing") wings. For low speeds the wings stick out nearly at right-angles. But for high speeds, the wings swing back.

Out of the ordinary

Aircraft designers are always experimenting with new designs, new engines, and new materials to see if they can build better planes Some planes, like the Lear Jet, are constructed out of composites, or reinforced plastics, rather than the usual aluminum. Some, like the Beech Starship, seem to be designed back-to-front, having the wing and engines at the rear and horizontal stabilizers in the nose.

Some have their wings swept forward rather than back. Others have X-shaped wings, scissor wings, and wings that swing back and forth – so-called swing-wings.

Plans for a space plane are well advanced. Early next century, it could even be carrying tourists to an orbiting space station! The pictures on these pages give a hint of how ingenious aircraft designers can be.

◀ Shuttle orbiter *Discovery* about to touch down after a space mission. The orbiter is part spacecraft, part aircraft. It takes off from a launch pad and is boosted into space by rockets. But it returns to Earth as a glider, landing on an ordinary runway.

► This plane has the most peculiar shape and is specially constructed to be invisible to radar. It is the F-117A "Stealth" plane.

▼ Here an X-29 experimental plane practices in-flight refueling. This remarkable plane has its wings swept forward, which reduces drag at high speeds.

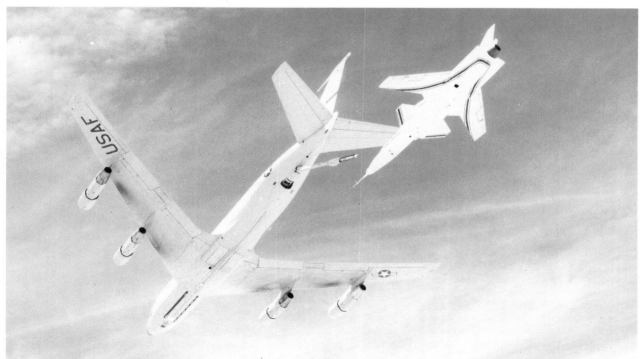

Helicopters and jump jets

Helicopters are the most versatile of all flying machines. They can operate from a small space, being able to take off and land vertically. In the air, they can fly in any direction, or simply hover in the same spot.

The most important feature of the helicopter is the rotor, or "rotary wing," on top of the fuselage. The blades of the rotor have an airfoil cross-section, like airplane wings. And, like airplane wings, they develop lift when they move through the air. When they spin fast enough, the lift they develop becomes greater than the weight of the helicopter, which rises into the air.

As the rotor spins in one direction, the body of the helicopter tries to spin in the opposite direction. To keep this from happening, a small rotor is fitted near the tail. It produces a sideways thrust that counteracts the body movement. Large helicopters like the Chinook have twin rotors, which rotate in opposite directions.

Q The Chinook does not have a tail rotor. Why doesn't its body spin around?

▼ The main features of a modern helicopter. Its 50-foot (15-meter) long rotor is driven by a shaft coupled to two gas-turbine engines. These are called turboshaft engines. The helicopter seats up to 20 people.

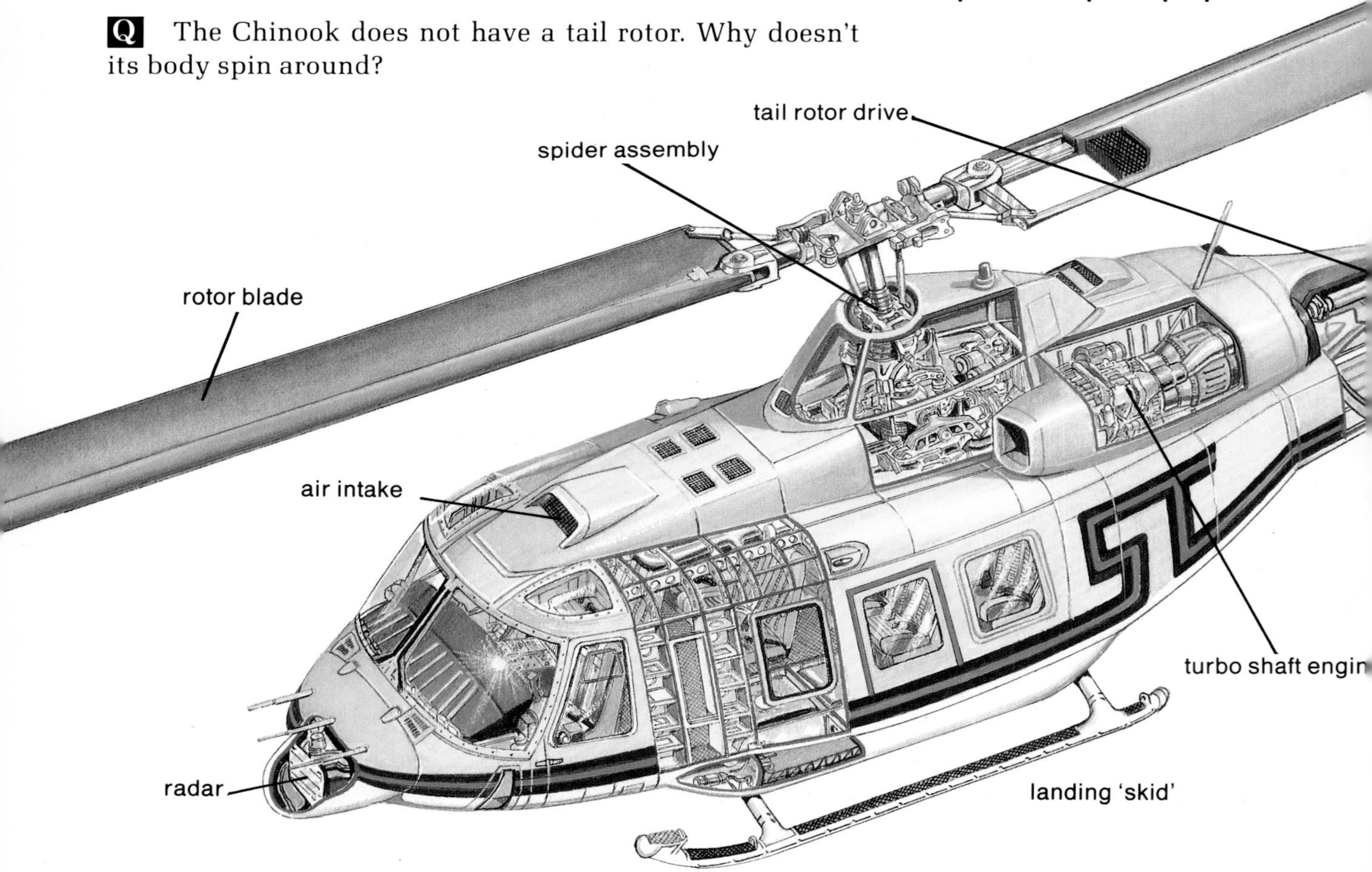

tail rotor drive

spider assembly

rotor blade

air intake

radar

turbo shaft engin

landing 'skid'

42

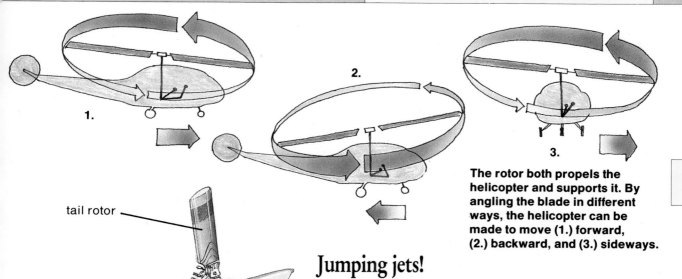

1.

2.

3.

The rotor both propels the helicopter and supports it. By angling the blade in different ways, the helicopter can be made to move (1.) forward, (2.) backward, and (3.) sideways.

43

tail rotor

elevator

Jumping jets!

A helicopter can take off and land in a small space, but it can travel only at relatively low speeds – up to about 200 mph (320 km/h). An ordinary jet plane can travel much faster, but it needs a long runway for take off and landing. It would be good if we could have an aircraft that could take off and land like a helicopter but have the speed of a jet. In fact, there is one – the Harrier. It is used by the U.S. armed forces in Europe.

The Harrier jump jet

The Harrier, nicknamed the jump jet, looks like an ordinary plane but is fitted with special swiveling nozzles that can change the direction of the exhaust jet from the engine. By deflecting its jet downward, the plane can move up and down vertically. In the air, the nozzles swivel so that they direct the jet exhaust backward, and the plane can then travel forward in the normal way. To keep it steady while it changes from vertical to horizontal flight, the Harrier fires jets of high-pressure air from nozzles in the nose, tail, and wing tips.

3
By Sea

◄ A cruise liner berthed in New York Harbor. Passengers now take to the seas for vacation cruises. The Bahamas, Caribbean, and the Greek islands are favorite destinations.

Sea-going ships carry the bulk of the world's cargo overseas. They can be built very large and can carry literally hundreds of thousands of tons of cargo at a time. No other form of transportation can match this. Until the middle of this century, ships also carried most people traveling overseas. But these days passengers prefer the speed of air travel, with journey times measured in hours rather than days.

Ships travel more slowly than just about any other means of transportation, such as the car, the train, and the plane. On the average, a cargo ship travels not much faster than you can pedal your bike!

Ships travel so slowly because of water resistance. To reduce this, some sea-going craft have been designed to skim over the surface rather than travel through it. These speedy "surface skimmers" include the hydrofoil and the hovercraft.

While these craft skim above the surface, others venture below it. The latest of these submarines are nuclear powered. Nuclear power is also used in some military ships, but it has not proved economical for civilian use.

► In the future ships may return to sails for propulsion. This modern Japanese-built tanker, the *Shin Aitoku Maru*, uses a mixture of wind power and diesel power for propulsion. The two sails are set by computer according to the direction of the wind.

46

▲ An Egyptian sailing boat of about 2000 BC. Models of boats like this have been found in ancient Egyptian tombs.

▲ A Viking longship of about AD 1000, propelled by oars as well as the sail. Longships were about 80 feet (24 meters) long and about 17 feet (5 meters) across.

The ship develops

No one knows exactly when people first began sailing the seas in ships. But we know that as early as 3000 BC, Crete was a seafaring nation with a large fleet of ships, which sailed and traded across the Mediterranean Sea. Other Mediterranean nations in time followed suit – the Phoenicians, the Greeks, and the Romans. Their ships were essentially similar. They were vessels known as galleys, propelled by one or more banks (levels) of oars. They also carried a square sail for use when sailing with the wind. Little basic change in ship design occurred until about a thousand years ago. That was when sailors in the Far and Middle East began using a triangular, or lateen, sail. This sail made it possible for vessels to sail almost into the wind as well as with the wind.

It was the first of a number of crucial developments that over the next few centuries transformed the ship into a true ocean-going vessel, tempting sailors to blaze new trails and discover "new worlds." Among these other developments were the stern rudder for steering; extra masts and sails; and raised platforms, or "castles," fore (at the front, or bow) and aft (at the rear, or stern).

By the 1400s most ships had three masts, the fore and main masts carrying square sails, and the rear, or mizzenmast, carrying a lateen sail. The hulls of the ships were built from wooden blanks butted edge to edge over a supporting framework. The joints were filled, or "caulked," with pitch to make them watertight.

The wooden sailing ship reached its most supreme form in the clipper of the mid-1800s. These graceful ships could reach speeds of up to 20 knots (about 23 mph, 37 km/h). They plied, for example, between America and the Far East carrying tea and other cargoes.

But by the time the clippers appeared on the scene, the days of the sail were really numbered. In the early 1800s steam power began to appear on the seas. The US vessel *Savannah*, propelled by side paddle wheels, crossed the Atlantic partly under steam in 1819. In 1845 the British ship *Great Britain* ushered in the modern age of ships. Its hull was made of iron and it was propelled by screw propeller.

By the turn of this century, the steam engine had given way to the steam turbine as the main source of power in large ships.

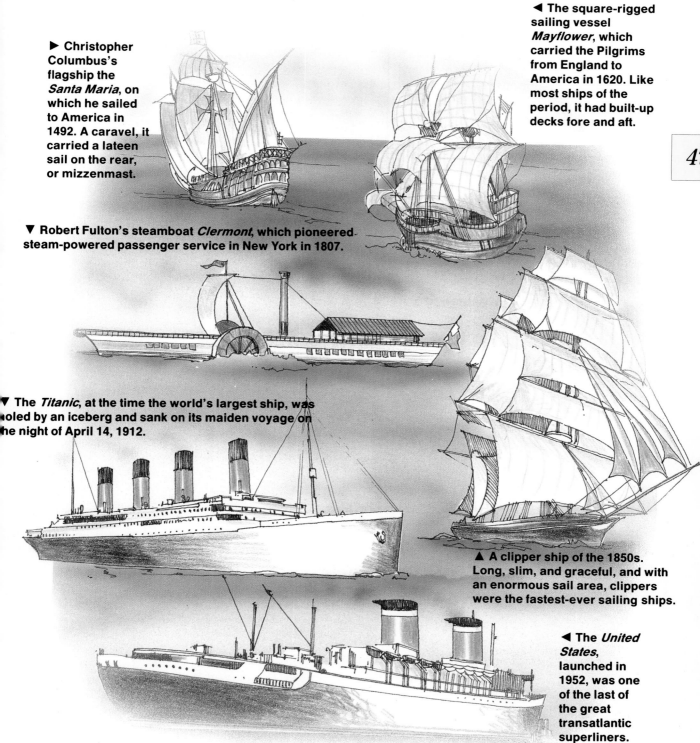

► Christopher Columbus's flagship the *Santa Maria*, on which he sailed to America in 1492. A caravel, it carried a lateen sail on the rear, or mizzenmast.

◄ The square-rigged sailing vessel *Mayflower*, which carried the Pilgrims from England to America in 1620. Like most ships of the period, it had built-up decks fore and aft.

47

▼ Robert Fulton's steamboat *Clermont*, which pioneered steam-powered passenger service in New York in 1807.

▼ The *Titanic*, at the time the world's largest ship, was holed by an iceberg and sank on its maiden voyage on the night of April 14, 1912.

▲ A clipper ship of the 1850s. Long, slim, and graceful, and with an enormous sail area, clippers were the fastest-ever sailing ships.

◄ The *United States*, launched in 1952, was one of the last of the great transatlantic superliners.

On the high seas

At any time of the night or day, tens of thousands of ships sail the seas. They vary greatly in size and purpose. Small fishing boats ply inshore waters; cruise liners take people on vacation; tugs maneuver larger vessels into and out of port; and merchant (non-naval) ships of many kinds provide vital trade links between nations.

U.S. merchant shipping is called the merchant marine. It includes over 600 ocean-going vessels with a total cargo-capacity, or deadweight tonnage, of 24 million tons. More than a third of these vessels are oil tankers.

Oil tankers are among the biggest ships afloat. Some of them are more than 1,000 feet (305 meters) long and are able to carry more than 500,000 tons of crude oil (petroleum). They are called VLCCs (Very Large Crude Carriers).

Q A VLCC may take three-quarters of a mile (1.2 km) to stop. Why?

Merchant fleets

The tanker is one kind of bulk carrier. Others may carry coal, ore, grain, or sugar. Container ships are another common type, the brainchild of the American Malcolm McLean

▼ *Norway*, the longest passenger liner there has ever been. Now based at Miami, Florida, she measures 1,035 feet (315.5 meters) long. Built in 1961, she was originally named *France*.

48

in 1955. They carry a variety of goods packed in standard-sized containers. The containers are loaded and taken off by specialized handling equipment.

Other interesting cargo vessels include the Ro-Ro and LASH types. In most cargo ships, cargo is loaded vertically by cranes and other handling equipment. In Ro-Ro (Roll on-Roll off) ships, cargo is loaded horizontally. Vehicle ferries operate in this way, for example. LASH stands for "Lighter Aboard SHip." In this method, cargo is packed into standard-sized barges, which are towed out to the ship and then lifted on board by cranes.

► **The container ship *Tokyo Bay*. It is specially built to carry all kinds of goods in standard-sized containers, which are loaded and taken off at the dockside by special built handling equipment.**

▼ **This interesting vessel, bristling with antennae, is pictured in the harbor at Cape Canaveral, Florida. It is a floating tracking station, used to track rockets and missiles from the Cape Canaveral launching sites.**

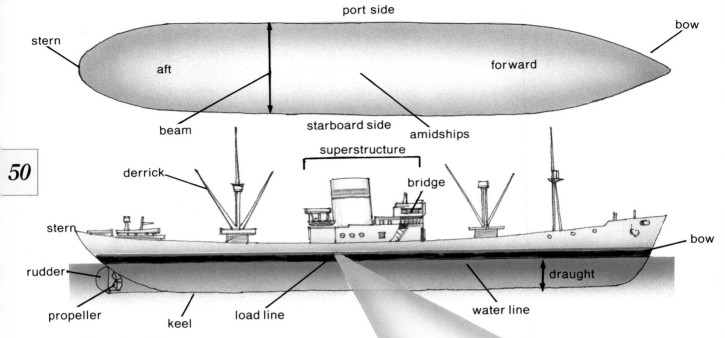

50

Basic principles

Most ships are made of steel and are very heavy. With a full cargo of crude oil, some tankers weigh more than half a million tons! Yet these ships float on water. How can that be?

When an object is placed in water, it loses weight. Pick up a brick and place it in a bucket of water, and you will feel the difference in weight. What is happening is that the water is exerting an upward force (upthrust) on the brick, which reduces its weight.

When you put the brick in water, it puts aside, or displaces, some of the water. If you weighed the amount of water displaced, you would find that it equalled the amount of weight the brick lost (equivalent to the upthrust of the water).

Q This scientific principle was discovered by a famous Greek mathematician more than 2,000 years ago. Who was it?

Staying afloat

Following on from the principle mentioned above, think what will happen if an object in water displaces a weight of water equal to its own weight.

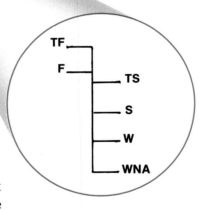

▲ **The Plimsoll line, or load line, has markings that show how heavily the ship may be safely loaded in different waters. (T = Tropical, F = Freshwater, S = Summer, W = Winter, N = North, A = Atlantic)**

Q **Can you explain them?**

The upthrust (force upward) of the water now equals the weight (force downward) of the object. In other words, the forces are balanced, and so the object doesn't sink. It floats.

This "law of flotation" is the basis of ship design. A ship is built with such a shape that it displaces an amount of water equal to its own weight.

Ship propulsion

Almost all ships are propelled by a propeller at the stern. In large naval ships and cruise liners, the propeller is turned by a steam turbine. The steam is produced in a boiler, in which water is heated by burning fuel, usually oil. The turbine drives the propeller shaft through a speed-reduction gearbox.

Most smaller craft are now powered by diesel engines. A few fast naval ships use gas turbines.

Q What other means of transportation use **(A)** diesel engines, **(B)** gas turbines for propulsion?

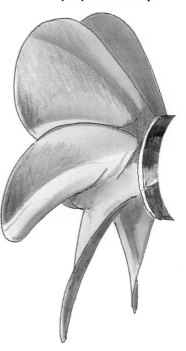

▼ A ship's screw propeller. The Swedish-born American engineer John Ericcson invented the screw propeller in 1836. It is usually made of manganese bronze, a strong, corrosion-resistant alloy. When it turns, it accelerates a stream of water backward. This sets up a thrust forward by reaction, and this thrust propels the ship.

51

◄ Ship-shape. This is an aerial view of the liner *Norway*. Most ships are of similar shape, with slender bows (front) so they experience less resistance when moving through the water.

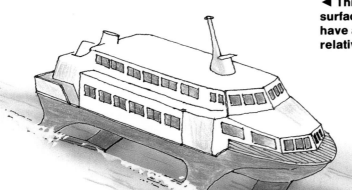

◀ This hydrofoil is fitted with what are called surface-piercing foils. In cross-section they have a V-shape. This design is best for relatively calm, inland waterways.

52

▼ This hydrofoil is fitted with horizontal, fully submerged foils. The Boeing Jetfoil has foils like this. The front one is used for steering the craft. This design is best for sea-going vessels.

Surface skimmers

We have seen earlier (page 36) how an airplane's wings develop lift when they travel through the air.

We can use the same principle to design boats that "fly" through the water. What we do is attach underwater "wings" to the hull. Then, when the boat travels through the water, the wings develop lift and rise. They gradually lift the hull out of the water. The boat can now travel much faster.

Q Why can the boat travel faster?

Hydrofoils

The proper name for the underwater wings is foils or hydrofoils – the name often given to boats fitted with them. Hydrofoils are now in widespread use for passenger service throughout the world. They have a typical cruising speed of about 43 knots (50 mph, 80 km/h).

The most advanced hydrofoil is the Boeing Jetfoil, which has fully submerged foils. It is computer-controlled and is driven by water jets. Water is taken in through a scoop in the rear foil and then pumped out of twin nozzles as high-speed jets.

WORKOUT

Each nozzle of the Boeing Jetfoil's water-jet system discharges 400 gallons (1,500 liters) of water per second. How much water does the boat discharge on a 20-mile (32-km) journey? (Assume it travels all the way at its cruising speed, 43 knots.)

Hovercraft

Another kind of surface-skimming craft looks nothing like a hydrofoil, more like a huge rubber dinghy. It does not need the typical hull of a boat because it rides almost completely out of the water on a "cushion" of air. It is usually called a hovercraft or ACV (air-cushion vehicle).

Freed from the drag of the water, hovercraft can move very fast. An experimental US Navy hovercraft (or SES – surface effect ship) has reached a speed of over 90 knots.

Q What is this speed in mph (km/h)?

Lift and propulsion

The air cushion on which hovercraft glide is produced by a powerful fan. A flexible rubber "skirt" around the bottom of the craft prevents the air from leaking away from the cushion too quickly.

For propulsion, hovercraft use backward-facing "pushing" propellers. They are steered either by swiveling the propellers or by moving rudders on tail fins at the rear.

▲ **Driven by propeller, a hovercraft skims across the surface of the sea. Note that the propeller has swiveled round to steer the craft in a different direction.**

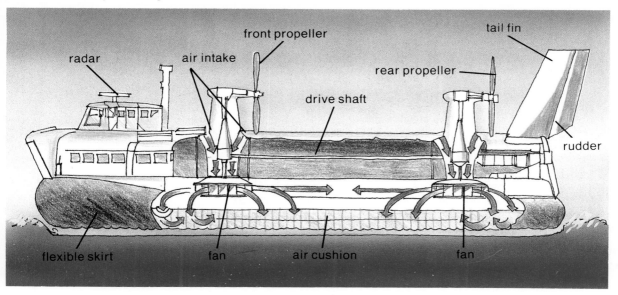

radar · air intake · front propeller · tail fin · rear propeller · drive shaft · rudder · flexible skirt · fan · air cushion · fan

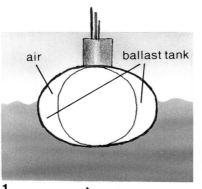

1.

2.

3.

Under the sea

In 1776 US inventor David Bushnell built a craft that could travel underwater. It was propelled by a hand-cranked propeller (see below). Over the two centuries since then, Busnell's craft developed into the most deadly fighting ship there is, the submarine.

The principle of submarining is simple. A submarine is fitted with ballast tanks, which can be filled with water and emptied when required. Look at the diagrams on the left.

1. On the surface, the ballast tanks are empty – that is, filled just with air – and the vessel is light enough to float.

2. Water is let into the tanks to make the vessel dive. Letting in water makes the vessel heavier, and so it sinks lower.

3. Letting in more water causes it to sink below the surface.

To surface, water is forced out of the ballast tanks with compressed air. The vessel becomes lighter until it is light enough to float on the surface.

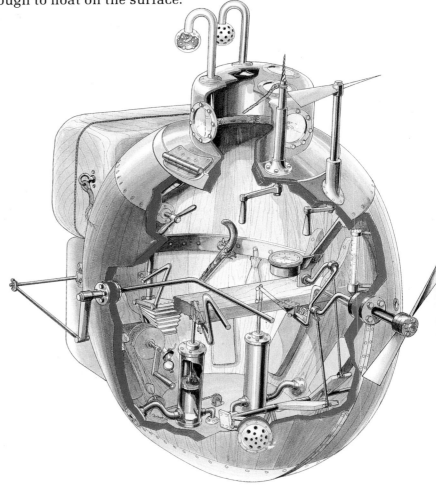

David Bushnell's submarine of 1776, called the *Turtle*. U.S. soldier Ezra Lee used it in an attempt to blow up the English warship *Eagle* in New York harbor. He planned to attach a charge of gunpowder to the hull of the ship with a screw device, but was foiled because the wooden hull was covered with copper.

Q **This episode took place during which war?**

Power and propulsion

All submarines are propelled by a propeller at the stern. They are steered left and right by means of a vertical rudder and movable horizontal fins, at the tail and on each side near the bow.

The latest submarines, which are large vessels up to 550 feet (170 meters) long, are nuclear powered. They have a nuclear reactor, which produces heat to boil water into steam. The steam drives turbines that spin the propeller.

Conventional (non-nuclear) submarines have two power sources. Underwater, the propeller is driven by an electric motor. On the surface, power is provided by a diesel engine. The engine also recharges the batteries.

Q Why can't a conventional submarine use its diesel engine to drive the propeller when it is traveling underwater?

▲ A submersible being lowered into the water from its support ship. This type of small submarine is now widely used, especially for marine research and for undersea construction work in the offshore oil industry.

◄ The nuclear-powered U.S. submarine *Dallas*, of the "Los Angeles" class. Nuclear "subs" like this are able to remain underwater for several months at a time. They can travel many hundred thousand miles without refueling.

56

Milestones

ABOUT 6000 BC Our ancestors began to domesticate animals and use them as beasts of burden to carry loads.

ABOUT 3000 BC The wheel was invented, and people began transporting loads in wagons. Sailing ships began sailing the seas.

ABOUT 2000 BC The Egyptians built swift chariots for carrying people, with spoked wheels much like modern wheels.

500 BC The Greeks developed the trireme, a fast ship propelled by three banks (levels) or oars.

AD 900-1000 The Vikings became a great seafaring nation, sailing in their longships.

1400s European adventurers embarked on exciting voyages of exploration. People began using horse-drawn coaches for long-distance travel by road.

1600s The first regularly scheduled stagecoaches appeared.

1769 Nicolas Cugnot in France built a steam-powered tractor.

1783 The Montgolfier brothers in France pioneered air travel when they built hot-air balloons.

1804 Richard Trevithick in Britain built the first steam-powered locomotive.

1807 Robert Fulton in the U.S. built the first successful steam-powered boat, *Clermont*.

1825 George Stephenson in Britain built the Stockton and Darlington Railway, the world's first public railroad. John Stevens ran the first experimental steam railroad in the U.S.

1852 Henry Giffard in France flew a steam-powered balloon – the first airship.

1869 The first U.S. transcontinental railroad was completed.

1885 Gottlieb Daimler and Karl Benz in Germany developed lightweight gasoline engines, and built the first motorcylce and motorcar.

1894 Charles Parsons in Britain built the first boat powered by steam turbine.

1897 Rudolf Diesel in Germany invented the oil engine named after him.

1900 Count Ferdinand von Zeppelin in Germany built his first airship. His huge zeppelins later helped promote transatlantic air travel.

1903 The Wright brothers in the U.S. made the first powered airplane flight.

1908 Henry Ford introduced his famous car, the Model T, or "Tin Lizzie."

1922 The cheapest car ever, the Red Bug Buckboard, was offered for sale in the U.S. for as little as $125.

1923 Juan de la Cierva in Spain first flew his autogiro.

1927 Charles Lindbergh made the first solo flight across the Atlantic in the *Spirit of St Louis*.

1930 British airman Frank Whittle took out a patent for a jet engine.

1937 The crash of the mammoth zeppelin *Hindenburg* in New Jersey in effect signaled the end of the airship era.

1939 Pan American Airways began the first transatlantic passenger service. The first jet plane, the Heinkel 178, flew in Germany. Igor Sikorsky in the U.S. flew the first successful single-rotor helicopter.

1947 Chuck Yeager became the first person to fly faster than the speed of sound in the rocket-powered Bell X-1. Howard Hughes made the first and only flight of his mammoth Hercules flying boat, nicknamed "Spruce Goose." Now on display at Long Beach, California, it has the largest wingspan of any aircraft ever built.

1950 The British *Comet* became the first jet airliner to go into regular service.

1952 The U.S. liner *United States* set the record speed for the transatlantic crossing of 10 hours 40 minutes. During this voyage she steamed the greatest distance ever covered by any ship in a days's run – 1,000 miles (1,609 km).

1954 The U.S. launched the first nuclear-powered submarine, *Nautilus*.

1955 Christopher Cockerell invented the hovercraft in Britain.

1964 The Japanese introduced the very fast "bullet trains."

1967 U.S. pilot William Knight set a world record speed for a fixed-wing aircraft of 4,520 mph (7,274 km/h) in a rocket-powered X-15A.

1969 The Boeing 747, the pioneering jumbo jet, made its maiden flight.

1971 The Apollo 15 astronauts used the first "car" on the Moon, the lunar rover, or Moon buggy.

1978 U.S. rider Donald Vesco set the world motorcycle speed record of 318.6 mph (512.7 km/h) on his twin engined, streamlined machine *Lightning Bolt*.

1979 The U.S. cyclist Bryan Allen made the first human-powered crossing of the English Channel in *Gossamer Albatross*.

1986 U.S. pilots Dick Rutan and Jeana Yeager flew the specially built aircraft *Voyager* non-stop around the world without refuelling. They took 9 days to complete the 25,000-mile (40,000-km) journey.

1990 In France a TGV high-speed train set a record railroad speed of 320 mph (515 km/h).

Glossary

AERODYNAMICS The study of the airflow around bodies traveling through the air and the forces that are set up.

AIR BRAKE A brake applied by compressed air. Trucks and trains have this kind of brake. The term also refers to a hinged flap on the wing of an airplane, which is raised to act as a brake after landing.

AIR-CUSHION VEHICLE (ACV) A vehicle that travels on a cushion of air, thereby reducing friction with the surface. The hovercraft is one type of air-cushion vehicle.

AIRFOIL The shape of an airplane wing: curved on top and flat underneath. This shape develops an upward force called lift when it travels through the air.

AIRPLANE A powered heavier-than-air craft that supports itself in the air by means of wings.

AIRSHIP A powered lighter-than-air craft that supports itself in the air by means of bags of a gas that is less dense than air. It is essentially a balloon with an engine.

AUTOGIRO An aircraft that is a cross between an airplane and a helicopter. It is propelled by a propeller and obtains lift from a spinning rotor.

BIPLANE An airplane with two sets of wings. Contrast MONOPLANE.

BLIMP A type of airship that does not have a rigid frame.

BRAKING The application of a mechanical device by the driver to retard the motion of a vehicle.

BULLET TRAIN A fast train whose front car has a streamlined shape resembling that of a bullet.

CLUTCH A unit in the transmission system of a car that connects the engine flywheel with the rest of the system. In cars with stick-shift transmission, the clutch disconnects the engine from the gearbox when the driver wishes to change gears.

COMPRESSION-IGNITION The principle on which the diesel engine works. Air becomes hot when it is compressed in the engine cylinders and ignites the fuel that is injected into the cylinder.

CONTAINER A standard-sized box in which cargo is carried. Containers can travel by truck, train, and ship, being transferred from one to the other by specialized handling equipment.

DELTA WING The triangular wing shape of some high-speed planes. It is named after the Greek letter capital delta.

DERAILLEUR GEARS Gears used on bikes that work by using a derailing mechanism to shift the chain between gear wheels of different sizes.

DIESEL-ELECTRIC The most common kind of locomotive in the U.S. It uses a powerful diesel engine to drive a generator to produce electricity, which is fed to electric motors that turn the wheels.

DIESEL ENGINE An internal combustion engine that works by compression-ignition. It uses a light oil as fuel.

DIFFERENTIAL A set of gears between the rear axles of a rear-wheel-drive automobile that allows the driving wheels to turn at different speeds, such as when the car is traveling around a corner.

57

58

DRAG A resisting force that a body experiences when it is traveling through the air or through water.

FLYWHEEL A heavy wheel on a rotating shaft that helps keep the shaft rotating smoothly.

FOUR-STROKE CYCLE The operating cycle of most gasoline and diesel engines, which repeats itself every four strokes (movements) of the pistons.

GAS TURBINE An engine in which power is produced when hot gases from a burning fuel spin a turbine. A jet engine is a kind of gas turbine.

GAUGE On the railroad, the distance between the two rails of the track. The usual, or standard, gauge is 4 feet 8 ½ inches (1.43 meters).

HELICOPTER A heavier-than-air flying machine that supports itself in the air, and is propelled by a spinning rotor.

HYDRAULIC BRAKES Brakes that work by liquid pressure.

HYDROFOILS Underwater "wings" attached to a boat hull that develop lift when they move through the water. They have a shape that is similar to that of an airfoil.

JET PROPULSION The principle on which a jet engine works. A jet engine produces a stream of hot gases, which shoot backward out of a nozzle. This sets up, by reaction, a force forward, called thrust. Jet thrust provides the propulsion for most modern airplanes. See TURBOFAN; TURBOJET; TURBOPROP.

JUMBO JET A large wide-bodied jet airliner, such as the Boeing 747, which can carry hundreds of passengers.

JUMP JET A plane that can take off and land vertically, particularly the Harrier, the most successful plane of this type.

LIFT An upward force developed by a plane's wings that supports the plane in the air. Hydrofoils also develop lift when they travel through the water.

MACH NUMBER A measure of the speed of an aircraft. It is the speed of the aircraft compared with the speed of sound. So Mach 2 means twice the speed of sound. It is named after an Austrian physicist Ernst Mach, a pioneer in aerodynamics.

MONOPLANE An airplane with one set of wings. Compare to BIPLANE.

NUCLEAR POWER Power produced by harnessing the energy given out when the nuclei (centers) of atoms (usually uranium) split.

PNEUMATIC TIRE A tire filled with air.

PROPELLER A screw-like device that most ships and some airplanes use for propulsion.

RACK A toothed rail used on steep mountain railroads. A pinion (toothed wheel) attached to the train meshes with the rack and enables the train to climb and descend slopes safely.

RADAR An electronic method of detecting ships at sea and aircraft in the air and measuring their distance. In radar (standing for radio detection and ranging), pulses of radio waves are bounced from craft and the echoes are displayed on a fluorescent screen.

ROTARY WING The rotor of a helicopter or autogiro, which provides lift when it spins.

SONAR A kind of "sound radar," which is used for detecting objects underwater and for underwater navigation.

SONIC BOOM A noise like thunder produced when an aircraft travels faster than the speed of sound.

SONIC SPEED The speed of sound, about 760 mph (1,200 km/h) at sea level. It becomes less with increasing height above sea level as the air becomes less dense.

STREAMLINED A term that describes objects that are specially shaped with flowing lines so that they can travel through the air or through water with the least resistance.

SUBMERSIBLE A small submarine.

SUPERSONIC Able to travel faster than the speed of sound.

SURFACE SKIMMER A craft that skims over the surface of the water, such as the hydrofoil and hovercraft.

SWING-WING A type of aircraft whose wings are pivoted and can be moved in different positions. It is properly called a variable-geometry wing.

TGV France's high-speed "bullet train" (*Train a Grande Vitesse*), which is even faster than the Japanese version.

THRUST A forward force such as that which is set up by a spinning propeller or jet of gases that propels an aircraft.

TRANSMISSION The system in a vehicle, ship, or other machine that transmits engine power to the driving wheels, propeller, and so on.

TRACTOR-TRAILER A truck whose body can swivel around a flexible coupling.

TURBOFAN The kind of jet engine used by most airplanes that has a huge fan in front.

TURBOJET The simplest kind of jet engine in which all the thrust is provided by a jet of gases.

TURBOPROP A kind of jet engine in which the turbine drives a propeller. Engine thrust comes both from the propeller and from the jet exhaust.

TURBOSHAFT The kind of jet engine used in most helicopters in which the turbine drives a shaft that spins the helicopter rotor.

ULTRASONIC WAVES Sound waves of very high frequencies that are beyond the range of human hearing.

VTOL An acronym for Vertical Take-Off and Landing. A term used to describe aircraft that can take off and land vertically, such as a helicopter.

WIND TUNNEL A tunnel in which air is circulated at different speeds by means of a powerful fan. New designs of aircraft, trains, cars, and other vehicles are now routinely tested in wind tunnels to ensure that they experience the least drag, or resistance, when they are in motion.

Answers

Page 14
1. **(F)** is correct – there are some 14,000 components.
2. Streamlined cars use less engine power in overcoming the resistance of the air. Therefore they use less fuel and are more economical to run.

Workout
On the pie chart cars occupy 270°, or 75 percent of the total number of motor vehicles (200 million). Therefore there are about 150 million cars in the U.S. There are about 43 cars per mile (27 cars per km). (You don't need to know the average length of a car, of course. This figure was given to confuse you!)

Page 16
Gasoline comes from crude oil, or petroleum. It is obtained when petroleum is distilled at an oil refinery.

Page 17
Another serious drawback of the gasoline engine is that it causes pollution. A car's exhaust system gives off a mixture of gases, including nitrogen oxides and carbon dioxide, also carbon monoxide, which is poisonous.. The nitrogen oxides get converted to acid in the air, leading to acid rain. The carbon dioxide helps contribute to the greenhouse effect, which is gradually making the world warmer.

Page 18
1. The ignition coil is an example of an electrical device called a transformer.
2. The natural circulation in water that is being heated is called convection. When a mass of water is heated, it expands and becomes lighter (less dense) than the surrounding water. It therefore rises, and colder, denser water moves in to take its place. This sets up convection currents.

Page 19
A gasoline engine contains hundreds of moving parts made of metal. If these were allowed to rub together, considerable friction would be set up. The engine would be noisy and would waste a lot of power in overcoming the friction. By oiling the moving parts, you coat them with a thin layer of oil. This layer prevents metal-to-metal contact, and reduces friction to a minimum, letting the moving parts run smoothly.

If an engine runs out of oil, the moving parts start rubbing together, and the friction between them creates heat. As the parts get hot, they expand. This forces them closer together and creates even greater friction. They soon expand so much that they become jammed and stop moving. The engine "seizes up."

Page 20
Vertical pipes discharge exhaust gases from the engine high into the air. This helps reduce pollution at ground level.

Page 21
(A) Having extra axles and extra wheels allows the weight of the load the truck is carrying to be distributed better. There is less pressure on each individual wheel. This reduces the wear and tear on both the tires and the road surface.

Workout
On the pie chart trucks occupy 81°, or 22.5 percent of the total number of motor vehicles (200 million). Therefore there are about 45 million trucks in the U.S. There are about 13 trucks per mile (8 trucks per km). (You don't need to know the average length of a truck, of course. This figure was given to confuse you!)

Page 23
In an air-cooled engine, the metal fins surrounding the cylinders provide a greater surface area for air to flow over, and this allows the heat to be removed more quickly.

Workout
On the pie chart motorbikes occupy 8°, or 2.2 percent of the total number of motor vehicles (200 million). Therefore there are about 4.4 million motorcycles in the U.S.

Page 28
The average number of passengers passing through each of New York Subway's stations is about 5,900 every day.

Page 31
On average a person's heart beats about 70 times a minute, so the time interval between heart beats is about 0.86 seconds. In that time the plane would travel 925 yards (846 meters).

Page 32
1. Balloons filled with either hot air or hydrogen will tend to rise in the air, because they are lighter, or rather less dense than the air. They experience an upthrust, or lifting force, because they displace (put aside) a weight of air greater than their own weight. This follows from Archimedes' famous principle.
2. Flyer's average speed was just under 7 mph (11 km/h).

Page 35
A Boeing 747 would take 15 hours to fly between Los Angeles and Sydney.

Page 37

The law of jet propulsion follows from Isaac Newton's third law of motion that states: "For every action, there is an equal and opposite reaction." The action (force backward) of the jet of gases shooting out of a jet engine sets up a reaction (force forward) that propels the engine.

Page 37

(A) Make an airfoil from a sheet of paper by bending it over and sticking the edges. Demonstrate the airfoil principle by hanging the airfoil from a pencil and blowing air over it.

(B) Make a paper glider by following these steps.

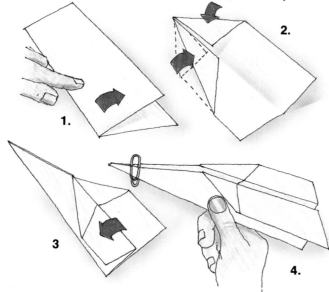

(C) To demonstrate the principle of jet propulsion, blow up the balloon, then let it go. The air escapes from the neck as a jet, setting up thrust to propel the balloon forward.

Page 38

(A) Moving the ailerons in this way causes the left wing to dip, the right wing to rise.

(B) Pulling on the control column raises the elevators and causes the nose of the plane to rise.

(C) Pressing the right rudder pedal moves the rudder to the right and causes the nose of the plane to shift to the right.

Page 42

The two rotors of the Chinook rotate in opposite directions. One tries to spin the body of the helicopter in one direction, while the other rotor tries to spin it in the opposite direction. The two effects cancel out, so no tail rotor is needed.

Page 48

A very large oil tanker is very heavy and has great inertia. This means that it is difficult to change its state of motion. A lot of effort is needed to get it moving, and a lot of effort is needed to slow it down once it is moving. The slowing-down process takes so long because you can't fit good brakes to a ship! You have to rely on reverse engine power and water resistance for braking.

Page 50

1. The famous Greek mathematician was Archimedes, who first stated the principle that the apparent loss in weight of an object when immersed in a liquid equals the weight of the liquid displaced.

2. Fresh water has less density than salty seawater. So the ship needs to ride lower in the water to displace its own weight of water. It doesn't matter that it rides lower in the water because freshwater lakes and rivers don't experience huge waves. On the other hand, the ship must ride higher out of the water in winter on the North Atlantic, where it is likely to be lashed by storms and huge waves.

Page 51

(A) Diesel engines are widely used for powering trucks and locomotives, and some cars.

(B) Gas turbines are most widely used for powering aircraft in the form of jet engines for airplanes and turboshaft engines for helicopters. A few locomotives are also powered by gas turbines.

Page 52

A boat riding on its foils can travel faster because its hull is raised above the surface and therefore experiences no resistance from the water. Water resistance is the main reason why water transport is so slow.

Workout

The Boeing Jetfoil discharges 1,152,000 gallons (4,320,000 liters) of water from its twin jet nozzles on a 20-mile (32-km) voyage.

Page 53

Using the figures for equivalent knots-mph (km/h) given on page 52, 90 knots is equivalent to nearly 105 mph (169 km/h).

Page 54

The first submarine attack took place during the Revolutionary War.

Page 55

A diesel engine needs to take in air from the atmosphere to burn its fuel. It therefore can't be used underwater.

For further reading

Bailey, Mark.
Cars, Trucks, and Trains.
Raintree Steck-Vaughn, Austin, Texas. 1988.

Baker, D.
I Want to Fly the Shuttle.
Rourke, Vero Beach, FL. 1990.

Cain, Wilma.
Story of Transportation.
Gateway Press, Grand Rapids, MI. 1988.

Keaton, Phyllis.
Buggies.
Macmillan, New York, NY. 1988.

Lake, A.
Pony Express.
Rourke, Vero Beach, FL. 1988.

Mellet, Peter.
Transportation.
Gareth Stevens, Milwaukee, WI. 1989.

Stewart, G.
Rivermen
Rourke, Vero Beach, FL. 1988.

Tames, Richard.
Amelia Earhart.
Childrens Press, Chicago, IL. 1990.

Tuttle, Liza.
A Multicultural Portrait of Railroads.
Marshall Cavendish, New York, NY. 1994.

Yepsen, Roger.
City trains: Moving Through America's Cities by Rail.
Macmillan, New York, NY. 1993.

Index

Numbers in *italics* refer to illustrations

aerodynamics 57
aileron *38, 39*
air brake 21, 57
air-cushion vehicle 53, 57
airfoil 36, 37, 42, 57
airplanes *30-41*, 57
air resistance 36
airscrew 37
airship 32, 57
American standard locomotive 24, 25
Amtrak 26, *27*
autogiro 57
automobile, see car

balloon 9, *31*
Beech Starship 40
Bell X-1 32, *33*
Benz, Karl 12, 13
Best Friend of Charleston 24
Big Boy locomotive 24, *25*
biplane 32, 57
Bleriot, Louis
blimp 57
body shell 14
Boeing 247 32, 33
Boeing 727 34
Boeing 747 32, *33, 35*, 36
Boeing 767 35
brakes *19*, 21, 57
bullet train 24, 57
Bushnell, David 54

cablecar *29*
canoe *8*
car 12-19
caravel 47
car systems *14, 15*
carburetor 19, 57
chassis 14, 20
Chinook 42
clipper 46, 47

clutch 57
Comet 32, 33
compression-ignition 57
compressor 337
Concorde *6, 7*
connecting rod *16*
Constellation 32, *33*
container 48, 49, 57
container ship 48, *49*
control column 38
cooling system *18*
crankshaft *16*, 17
cruise liner *44*, 45
Cugnot, Nocolas 12
Curtiss, Glenn 32
Curtiss Jenny 32, *33*

Dallas 55
Daimler, Gottlieb 12
Dakota 32, *33*
DC-3 32, *33*
DC-10
delta wing 57
derailleur gears 57
De Witt Clinton 24, 25
diesel engine 17, 20, 21, 27, 55, 57
diesel-electric 27, 57
diesel locomotive 27
differential 57
Discovery 40
disk brake *19*
distributor *18*
drag 36, 58
drum brake *19*
Duryea brothers 12

electric locomotive 27
elevators 38, 39
engine, car 16-19
Ericcson, John 51

final drive 19, 58
flaps 38, *39*
float plane 32, 33
Flyer 32, *33*
flying doctor 35
flywheel 58
Ford, Henry 12, 13
four-stroke cycle *16*, 17, 57

France 48
fuel injection 19, 58

galley 46
gas turbine 27, 43, 51, 58
gas-turbine locomotive *27*
gasoline engine 12, 16-19
gauge, rail *26*, 58
gearbox 15, 19, 21, 58
gliding *8*
Golden Flyer 32, *33*
Great Britain 46

Hallidie, Andrew 29
hang-gliding *9*
Harrier *43*
Hartsfield Atlanta International Airport 34
helicopter *42, 43*, 58
horizontal stabilizer *38, 39*
horseback riding *9*
hovercraft *53*
hydraulic brake 58
hydrofoil *52*, 58

ignition coil *18*
ignition system *18*

jet engines *37*
Jetfoil *52*
jet propulsion 32, 58
John Bull 24, *25*
jumbo jet 32, *33, 34, 35*, 58
jump jet *43*, 58

LASH 49
law of flotation 51
Lear Jet 40
Lee, Ezra 54
lift 36, 58
load line *50*
locomotives 24, 27
longship *46*
lubrication system 19, 58

Mach number 58
maglev system 28
Mallard 24, *25*
Mayflower 47

merchant ships 48, 49
Model T *13*
monoplane 32, 58
monorail *28*
Montgolfier brothers 31
motorcycles *22, 23*
Mt. Pilatus rack railroad *29*
muffler 15

New York Subway 29
National Railroad Passenger
    Corporation 26
Norway 48, 51
nuclear power 55, 58

O'Hare International Airport 34
oil 19
Olds, Ransome. E. 13
Oldsmobile 13

pantograph 27
piston *16*, 17
planes, see airplanes
pneumatic tire 58
propeller 36, 37, *51*, 58
propeller shaft 14, 19, 58

rack railroad 28, *29*, 58
radar 58
radiator *15, 18*
railroads 24-29
Rocket 25
rocket plane 32, *33*
Ro-Ro 49
rotary wing 58
rudder *38, 39*

sailing *9*, 10
sailing ships *46, 47*
Santa Maria 47
Savannah 46
semitrailer 20
screw propeller 46, *51*
Shin Aitoku Maru 45
ships 44-51
shock absorber 14
slats 39
sonar 58
sonic boom 59

sonic speed 59
space planes 40
space shuttle *40*
spark plug *16*, 17
spoilers *39*
stagecoach *12*
standard gauge 26
Stanley Steamers 12
stealth plane *41*
steam car 12
steam tractor 13
steering 19, 59
Stephenson, George 24, 26
Stevens, John 24
Stourbridge Lion 24
streamlined 14, 59
streamliners 24, 25
submarine *54, 55*
submersible *55*, 59
Supermarine S6B 32, *33*
supersonic 59
surface effect ship (SES) 53
surface skimmer 52, 53, 59
suspension 14, 15, 19, 59
swing-wing *40*, 59

tail (airplane) 38, 39
tanker 48
TGV 59
thrust 37, 59
Tin Lizzie 12, 13
Titanic 47
Tokyo Bay 49
Tomcat *40*
track, railroad 26
tractor-trailer 59
transcontinental railroad 24
transmission 59
Trevithick, Richard 24, 25
Tristar 34
truck tractor 20
trucks 20-21
turbine *37*
turbofan *37*, 59
turbojet 37, 59
turboprop 37, 59
turboshaft engine 42, 59
Turtle 54

ultrasonic waves 59
United States 47
upthrust 50

variable-geometry wing 40
V-engine 17
vertical stabilizer *38, 39*
VLCC 48
VTOL 59

wind tunnel 59
wind-surfing *8*
wing (airplane) 36
Wright brothers 32

X-1 32, *33*
X-29 *41*

Yeager, Chuck 32